THE EMPOWERED
HIGHLY SENSITIVE PERSON

the
EMPOWERED
HIGHLY
SENSITIVE
PERSON

A WORKBOOK
to Harness Your Strengths
in Every Part of Life

AMANDA CASSIL, PhD

ROCKRIDGE PRESS

To my partner, best friend, and fiercest advocate, Ben.
You make me a better version of myself.
Thank you.

For general information on our other products and services or to obtain technical support, please contact our Customer Care Department within the United States at (866) 744-2665, or outside the United States at (510) 253-0500.

Rockridge Press publishes its books in a variety of electronic and print formats. Some content that appears in print may not be available in electronic books, and vice versa.

TRADEMARKS: Rockridge Press and the Rockridge Press logo are trademarks or registered trademarks of Callisto Media Inc. and/or its affiliates, in the United States and other countries, and may not be used without written permission. All other trademarks are the property of their respective owners. Rockridge Press is not associated with any product or vendor mentioned in this book.

Interior and Cover Designer: Heather Krakora
Art Producer: Tom Hood
Editor: Vanessa Ta
Production Editor: Andrew Yackira
Author photo by Ben Cassil

ISBN: Print   978-1-64611-456-6
        eBook 978-1-64611-457-3

R0

CONTENTS

INTRODUCTION vii

HOW TO USE THIS WORKBOOK ix

CHAPTER ONE: The Highly Sensitive Person 1

CHAPTER TWO: Everyday Life and Social Situations 11

CHAPTER THREE: Relationships 49

CHAPTER FOUR: Work 85

CHAPTER FIVE: Health and Self-Care 105

CHAPTER SIX: Deeper Work 133

Resources 157

References 158

Index 160

INTRODUCTION

Maybe you're perpetually exhausted and people describe you as "high-strung." You may struggle to keep up with housework or feel oddly depleted by your job. As you go through your day, interactions with your colleagues may leave you feeling full of self-doubt and on the verge of tears. Even positive feedback from your boss may leave you feeling confused, as though you just got in trouble. You may find it hard to focus or think clearly during the latter half of the day or get headaches when stressed. Your favorite part of the day might be those 30 minutes by yourself between activities, when you get to rest in a quiet, dark space. "What am I doing wrong?" you wonder to yourself. "Other people don't seem to struggle like I do."

Surviving in an overwhelming world and assuming something is "wrong" may be a common experience for you, a highly sensitive person (HSP). Thankfully this is not the case. Context and knowledge can make all the difference in how you experience the world.

I first heard the term *highly sensitive person* during my clinical internship at Caltech over 10 years ago. As an HSP, or highly sensitive person, I was intrigued that this trait had a name and was a common experience for a significant portion of the population. At the time, there was limited information on the topic, with Dr. Elaine Aron almost exclusively providing resources. Dr. Aron is a psychologist who began studying the HSP trait in 1991 and published *The Highly Sensitive Person* (1996). Since I learned of the trait, I have followed the emerging research about HSPs and learned anecdotally, as the majority of clients I work with are highly sensitive.

As a licensed clinical psychologist, I work with women and underrepresented minorities in STEM fields (science, technology, engineering, and math). I have had the privilege of helping clients understand the HSP trait and leverage it into a key factor for their success. When I first meet HSP clients, they are usually experiencing some form of depression or anxiety as they function in the high-pressure environments of STEM. Over time, as they do their work in therapy, they blossom and thrive. Typically this includes an increase in confidence, changes in body language, more fulfilling relationships, and improved quality of life. This does not mean that things become easy but that these HSPs now have more tools to use when life throws inevitable challenges at them.

This book is based on the research literature as well as my observations of consistent themes for HSPs through my work as a psychologist. The exercises come from questions and practices I give my clients every day. Some of them will work for you and others won't, and that's okay. As you try them, you can decide which tools to take with you and incorporate into regular usage so that you, too, can blossom and thrive.

HOW TO USE THIS WORKBOOK

This book is designed to give you a broad overview of common experiences that affect HSPs. Consistent themes will be explored in each chapter, such as past experiences and common challenges. Exercises will balance reflecting on the past, assessing the present, and planning for the future. You are welcome to read straight through the book or to jump around based on your needs and interests. As is the nature of any workbook, there are limitations to how comprehensive each section can be, so a list of resources is provided at the end for you to continue your work beyond this book.

There are a few things to keep in mind as you read. First, every HSP experience is unique. So if something in this book does not resonate with you, that does not negate your experience. Generalities are helpful for understanding groups but can miss the nuances of the individual. Your best bet is to trust your knowledge of how things have been for you and continue to research writings from other authors for diversified perspectives.

Second, any time you are doing work around past experiences, there is a risk of triggering or worsening mental health conditions. Be sure to seek help from a trained professional near you if you find yourself triggered by any of the exercises in this book. Many therapists will be more than happy to facilitate your journey through self-help exercises like those found in this workbook.

Finally, most of the exercises in this book can be repeated. Flip through and scan some of the exercises as you prepare to do the work to see what might be a useful approach for you. Some people prefer using a journal, writing on their computer or phone, or photocopying the exercises. The most important thing is to engage with the workbook in a way that is meaningful and useful for you.

This is not likely a book that you will cruise through quickly. Give yourself time to space out the exercises, digest the information, and circle back to previous exercises. Getting to know yourself is similar to getting to know a friend. It can be fun, exciting, and tiring and involves a flood of new information that sometimes needs to be revisited. You will be holding this new information in dialogue with old experiences you have had, and that will be an ever-evolving conversation. It is a fluid process that will never be fully done—and that's a beautiful thing.

CHAPTER ONE

The Highly Sensitive Person

Whether the label highly sensitive person (HSP) is new to you or you have been familiar with it from its inception over 20 years ago, this chapter will provide an overview of what it means to be an HSP. Throughout this workbook, you will find common challenges and advantages unique to the HSP experience in family, relationships, work, health, and social settings.

This book may be a journey of exciting discovery or one fraught with tension; most likely it will be a little of both. Give yourself space to respond to whatever emotions may arise as you explore this trait. The process of self-discovery and insight is never straightforward or smooth. For the information that resonates with you, take it in, digest it, and integrate it into your understanding of yourself. For the information that does not, feel free to let it go.

What Does It Mean to Be Highly Sensitive?

The HSP trait is a combination of four principles: an increased **depth of processing**, a tendency to be more **easily overstimulated**, a higher level of **emotional intensity**, and increased awareness of **environmental subtleties** due to sensory sensitivities when compared to non-HSP groups (Aron, 2010). Each of these will be discussed in more depth in future chapters and paired with exercises to help you assess and respond to how these present in your life.

DEPTH OF PROCESSING

HSPs are deep thinkers. This makes them good at considering all sides of a scenario or being in tune with trends, world events, the meaning of life, and contextual layers of experiences. Deep thinking can make HSPs slow to make decisions or come to conclusions. This quality can manifest as high conscientiousness, mindfulness of others, awareness of long-term consequences, high levels of insight, and needing time for reflection.

Research has shown associations between the HSP trait and increased activity in brain structures related to cognition, sensory processing, attention, and emotional information processing (Greven et al., 2019). These brain studies, along with a proposed genetic correlation, point to an underlying biological basis for the HSP trait. As HSPs take in information from the world around them, they are digesting that information thoroughly, as evidenced by the measured brain activity. But this depth of processing, while highly valuable, can be exhausting and lead the HSP to feel overstimulated.

EASE OF OVERSTIMULATION

Along with increased brain activity, HSPs have increased reaction times, activity in brain structures that provide high-order visual processing, and activation of brain structures that process sensory integration and awareness (Greven et al., 2019). That means HSPs are more impacted by input from their five senses and can become overstimulated as a result (Aron, 2010). This overstimulation can result from high-intensity stimuli (e.g., a loud bang or strong odor) or prolonged low-intensity stimuli (e.g., a soft ticking sound in the background).

When an HSP does not have good coping strategies, overstimulation can result in chronic stress, anxiety, and avoidance behaviors. When well managed, high stimulation can allow HSPs to thoroughly take in enjoyable parts of life, like fine food, delicate scents, or the beauty of nature, and to thrive in fields that require deep processing, like art and science.

EMOTIONAL INTENSITY

HSPs have an increased emotional response to both positive and negative emotional experiences when compared to non-HSPs (Aron, 2010). This increased emotional response can look like being moved to tears by joy, gratitude, or relief. Conversely, HSPs may be more negatively impacted by violent TV shows, social injustice, or rudeness. HSPs are also more aware of and affected by the emotions of others. HSPs can be like sponges, absorbing the positive or negative moods coming from other people.

HSPs often take significantly longer than non-HSPs to "get over" something socially or to process significant life events (both positive and negative). Research has shown increased activity in brain structures that process emotions and empathy for HSPs (Greven et al., 2019). This brain activity means HSPs are often highly aware of the emotional states of others, which can be described as "intuition." HSPs are sometimes able to discern the emotional state of another person better than that person can.

SENSORY SENSITIVITY AND ENVIRONMENTAL SUBTLETIES

An HSP's sensory sensitivity can make them highly perceptive of subtle changes in their environment. This perceptiveness is related more to how the sensory information is processed in the brain than to the sensory organs themselves (Aron, 2010). In other words, when an HSP notices a rough texture, it is not because they have extra-sensitive fingers but because their brain structures are processing the information taken in by the fingers in a deeper way.

Sensory sensitivity and connection with subtlety awareness has also been supported in the research. HSPs showed increased neural activity when detecting minor changes rather than major changes (Greven et al., 2019). HSPs may notice subtle differences that others consider impossible or unlikely, such as a one- to two-degree change in temperature.

The full breadth of scientific discovery is beyond the scope of this book, but for those interested, two helpful overviews of the literature include an overview appendix chapter in Dr. Aron's 2010 publication, Psychotherapy and the Highly Sensitive Person, and a critical literature review by Greven et al. (2019). When looking up research on your own, know that HSP is termed sensory processing sensitivity (SPS) in the research literature.

HIGHLY SENSITIVE PEOPLE VS. INTROVERTS, EXTROVERTS, AND EMPATHS

Social situations can be overwhelming to HSPs, as they continually process a lot of data: the emotions of others, microexpressions, implicit messages, and contextual cues in their environment. HSPs often use coping mechanisms in overstimulating social situations, like hanging back to observe, leaving early, and decompressing afterward. These behaviors might be incorrectly labeled as introversion when in fact these are separate traits.

Introversion and extroversion, as defined by the popular Myers-Briggs Type Indicator, describe psychological preferences for what energizes a person. Introverts may enjoy but become exhausted by a night out with friends. They tend to draw energy from solo activities and engaging with ideas, sometimes with one or two close friends. Extroverts, on the other hand, may enjoy a night in with a good book but feel restless to get out of the house and interact with people. And while many HSPs identify as introverts (about 70 percent; Aron, 2010), the HSP trait and introversion/extroversion measure different things. Again, the HSP's sensory sensitivity looks at how information is processed while introversion/extroversion looks at where one puts their attention and from where they draw energy.

A term often used interchangeably with HSP is *empath*. A key marker of HSPs is the emotional intensity they can feel and their awareness of the emotional experiences of others. Some people use the terms *HSP* and *empath* interchangeably while others attribute a spiritual component to empaths separate from HSPs, and even others see empaths as a subset of HSP who experience HSP traits to an even deeper degree than other HSPs. It can be helpful to ask for clarification when someone uses the term *empath*. To date, this is not a scientifically researched concept.

HSPs come in all forms, and everyone experiences social environments differently. Asking questions about what energizes you, what exhausts you, what makes you nervous, and what fulfills you can help you tease out which labels are useful in communicating your preferences and needs to others. It can also help you as you plan ahead and build helpful coping skills around potentially draining social situations.

Highly Sensitive People and Society

Cultural ideals in any society have a significant impact on HSPs. As an HSP, you might recall feeling that your skills and abilities were overlooked because someone who seemed less sensitive, less attuned, and more outgoing was viewed as being better suited to a task. Susan Cain (2012) provides a helpful example of this when discussing the history of extroversion in the American entrepreneurial spirit. She connects this to implicit and explicit messages one might receive in the business world around networking or prioritizing presentation skills. Cain acknowledges that while these can be useful skills, prioritizing them often comes with minimizing other skills in the workplace. But the pressure to be extroverted doesn't stop with business. Cultural ideals can be shaped by many factors. Here are some examples that can be challenging for HSPs:

» High-density cities (e.g., New York City, Beijing, Mumbai)

» Loud events (e.g., concerts, parties, nightclubs)

» Valuing fame and influence (e.g., seeing public speaking or performances as more valuable than teaching)

» Decision fatigue (e.g., too many options in the grocery store)

» Social expectations (e.g., while in college, being expected to stay up late, indulge in alcohol and caffeine, and tolerate noisy dorms)

» Valuing busyness (e.g., praising people for insufficient sleep due to working too hard)

» Gendered messages (e.g., "men don't cry")

Can you think of additional examples from your culture that may provide a sense of tension between what is valued by society and what works best for you?

The goal of this book is not to "cure" you of being highly sensitive but to help you learn how to leverage being an HSP. With any skill or trait, learning to work with it involves an accurate assessment of the pros and cons, allowing you to make informed decisions moving forward. This process will inevitably bring up feelings of frustration, sadness, and disappointment—emotions that often come with the process of growth. As you grieve and let go of what you do not (and cannot) have, it can open up space to appreciate what you do have. The activities in this book will hopefully strike a balance between assessing, grieving, and embracing your trait as you move toward thriving.

A helpful exercise when you get discouraged is to think about the value that HSPs have in society (even when it is not fully recognized). Many gifted artists, philosophers, musicians, researchers, doctors, healers, and teachers have significantly impacted the lives of others when they learned how to work within the limitations afforded by their sensitivities.

Understanding Your Past

HSPs often struggle with feeling different. They recall hearing messages such as "you are too sensitive," "this shouldn't bother you so much," and "just get over it already." These messages can contribute to an internalized sense of shame around the trait. For example, perhaps you were the HSP child who felt overwhelmed by the sounds and smells in the school cafeteria or the one who shied away from high-conflict family members. These experiences could have resulted in feeling marginalized by peers or adults who didn't share your HSP experience.

Each chapter in this book will feature sections that connect back to early childhood experiences and help you understand how these messages can become templates through which you understand current and future experiences. Reworking these harmful templates can be hard and painful yet liberating and empowering. The term *intersectionality* will be used to encourage you to reflect on how the different identity pieces you hold (e.g., gender, race, income level) interact with one another and your identity as an HSP.

If you currently have an HSP child, you may find parallels between the work of reflecting on your past as an HSP child and supporting your HSP child in the present. Many HSP children are highly observant and intuitive. When an HSP child becomes overstimulated and feels overwhelmed, their reaction may seem excessive. But to the child it *is* a big deal, and ignoring or dismissing the emotion can result in deep hurt. HSP children can have strong reactions to stimuli, such as tension among family members, being left alone too long or too early, feeling unsupported, and not receiving reassurance. When struggling with this trait, the HSP child may show higher stress levels than their peers, exhibit high levels of nervousness or anxiety, have trouble transitioning between tasks, and want to avoid overwhelming situations.

Chapter 3 will go into additional depth on HSP children in families. A couple of helpful guidelines to keep in mind are that HSP children often respond well to gentle correction and may feel deeply wounded by strong or intense punishments; that HSP children often benefit from discussions around why certain rules are in place or why they are being punished; and that HSP children can handle intense emotions if they have a trusted adult who can help them contextualize and process these emotions. Reflecting on your own childhood may highlight areas where these needs were missed as well as meaningful advocates you found along the way. It may also help you identify and support the needs of an HSP child in your life.

Highly Sensitive Person Checklist

The standard measurement for the HSP trait is Dr. Aron's "Are You Highly Sensitive?" test (1996). If you haven't done so already, you can take the interactive test at hsperson.com. Here is a condensed checklist of the four principles of the HSP trait to help you understand your individual HSP characteristics. Check the boxes that apply to you.

DEPTH OF PROCESSING

☐ I tend to think deeply about decisions, which can mean I am slow at making decisions.

☐ I enjoy spending time in reflection on complex topics.

☐ I try hard to live according to my beliefs.

☐ I like to give tasks my best efforts and strongly dislike making mistakes.

EASE OF OVERSTIMULATION

☐ I benefit from solitude or quiet, dark environments when I get overstimulated, as it helps me calm down.

☐ I find myself overwhelmed, annoyed, or exhausted by intense sights, sounds, smells, tastes, or textures.

☐ I find having multiple deadlines, being observed, or chaotic environments particularly distressing.

EMOTIONAL INTENSITY

☐ I am aware of and affected by the moods of other people.

☐ I tend to be mindful of how to help others feel more comfortable in a situation.

☐ I find myself deeply moved by sights, sounds, smells, tastes, or textures that I find pleasing.

☐ I feel calmer when my life is predictable and moves at an even pace.

SENSORY SENSITIVITY

☐ I pick up on subtle changes in my environment.

☐ I am easily affected by substances (e.g., caffeine) or internal stimuli (e.g., sensation of hunger).

☐ I have been told I am highly observant.

As you can see by the boxes you checked, there can be great variation in the way the HSP trait is expressed from person to person. Perhaps you checked most of the boxes in the Ease of Overstimulation category but few to none in the Depth of Processing category. Throughout the remainder of the book, you will learn more about how to harness your individual HSP characteristics in a way that is empowering, particular to your specific needs, and aligned with your individual goals.

CHAPTER RECAP

As you move through this book, remember that no two HSP experiences are the same. You will resonate deeply with some exercises and find others less helpful. Take what works for you and let go of the rest. Remember:

1. HSPs exhibit deep thinking, ease of overstimulation, emotional intensity, and sensory sensitivity to environmental subtleties.

2. Your identity as an HSP is simply one facet of who you are. Keep all parts of yourself in dialogue as you move through this book.

3. Some things (e.g., your responses) are within your control, and some things (e.g., societal structures) are not. Pick your battles accordingly, and be careful what you take responsibility for.

CHAPTER TWO

Everyday Life and Social Situations

Moving through life as a highly sensitive person can be exhausting, as one deeply processes countless emotions and stimuli. Tasks that non-HSPs see as simple or easy may end up overwhelming an HSP, leaving them feeling depleted or anxious. In this chapter, you will reflect on some aspects of everyday life as an HSP. The exercises will help you take stock of what works well for you, what does not, and what you may want to change. Toward this end, you will explore how to implement self-care and positive experiences and learn to evaluate and cope with negative experiences.

Highly Sensitive People and Everyday Life

Ideally, in day-to-day life, you experience enough stimulation to be motivated and engaged with what you are doing but not so much that you are overwhelmed, anxious, or shut down. Not all stress is bad, and in fact stress can be beneficial when it activates or stimulates the central nervous system *just enough* to help you complete a task. Overstimulation occurs when stress impairs functioning.

Switching environments, tasks, and social contexts involves processing change physically, cognitively, and emotionally. HSPs often intuitively implement helpful strategies into their day-to-day functioning to cope with this processing, such as always carrying a jacket "just in case." These strategies help prevent overstimulation and keep you in optimal functioning. Shifting from unintentional to intentional coping can increase your confidence and ability to advocate for your needs or adapt to challenges when needed. Three intentional practices for HSPs are building transition time, following routines, and curating your environment.

TRANSITION TIME. Transitions allow you time to wind down from one activity in both thought processes and stimulation levels and switch to a new focus. Similar to a warm-up or cooldown when exercising, bodies need time to adjust. These transitions give you space to calm stimulation from one task before gearing up for the next—a practice that can be crucial in regulating stress levels.

Transitions might be as simple as taking a bathroom break between meetings at work or asking if dinner with a friend can be pushed back 30 minutes. The need for transition time comes up often around waking and sleeping routines for HSPs, who often benefit from unwinding at the end of the day before heading to bed through calming activities such as reading or journaling. Similarly, HSPs often prefer not to jump out of bed in the morning, so building in a 30-minute window where one might mentally prepare for the day can make a significant difference in stress levels.

ROUTINE. Routines help you know what to expect and allow you to run on muscle memory, thus helping you regulate stimulation levels. People are often more alert and focused when doing novel tasks, so if your body never knows what to expect, you are operating in a state of heightened attention for activities that do not need that level of attention. If you follow the same morning routine each day, then cognitive resources are not being used up on each of these little tasks. Those cognitive resources are then available for other tasks throughout the day. It is common for HSPs to occasionally evaluate their various routines for efficiency and simplicity.

CURATING ENVIRONMENTS. Curating your environment can help you manage daily stress, especially shaping relaxation spaces like bedrooms or living areas. Due to high levels of processing sensory information, HSPs are constantly fielding input from their environment. New or changing stimuli, chaotic surroundings, or offensive stimuli (e.g., harsh lighting or bad smells) lead to stimulation of the central nervous system. HSPs often dislike clutter in their living environments because their brains see each piece of clutter as a data point (or novel visual stimulus) that needs to be processed. Less novel visual stimuli result in less stimulation.

Curating shared space can be challenging. Good communication of your needs and the willingness to compromise are key. Be aware of how you respond to different colors, shapes, textures, spacing, lighting, sound, and scents. Use this awareness to create spaces that move you into (for a workspace) or out of (for a relaxation space) optimal stimulation. Even small adjustments, like tidying a stack of papers, can make a significant difference.

Assessing and Curating Your Environment

In this exercise, you will take a moment to assess how your environment affects you.

Take a minute to sit in a space in your home that you occupy regularly. Scan the space slowly, observing everything you take in with your five senses.

Notice how you feel both emotionally and physically. Make notes in the squares on page 14 of the things that inhibit and promote your relaxation based on your five senses. You might feel calm, restless, energetic, tired, tense, agitated, overwhelmed, or any number of things. Ideally, in places meant for relaxing (e.g., the living room or bedroom), the environment cues and supports this experience. Repeat this exercise in each living space that you occupy regularly.

	...THAT HELPS YOU RELAX?	...THAT DISRUPTS RELAXATION?
WHAT DO YOU SEE...	Ex: the color teal	Ex: clutter on the desk
WHAT DO YOU HEAR...	Ex: birds chirping	Ex: ticking clock
WHAT DO YOU SMELL...	Ex: candle	Ex: dirty clothes
WHAT DO YOU FEEL...	Ex: soft blanket	Ex: splinters on the handrail

Once you have assessed the space, take a moment to reflect on the list of disruptions. List the top three disruptive pieces and how each affects you.

Example: Clutter on the desk increases my anxiety because it feels like I have an incomplete task list.

1. _____

   _____

2. _____

   _____

3. _____

   _____

Now make a list of how you can change each of the stressful factors.

Example: Stack paperwork and mail into three piles—"to be filed," "shred," and "needs reply"—and sort them as I receive them.

1. _____

   _____

2. _____

   _____

3. _____

   _____

Finally, list the top three helpful stimuli. Keep these in mind when curating future spaces, and see these as resources to enjoy during stressful times. Knowing what is calming to you allows for better self-care; prioritize this when enjoying your space.

Example: Hearing the birds in the morning is relaxing. On days when I feel stressed, I can open the window while I enjoy my coffee to hear them even better.

1. _____

_____

2. _____

_____

3. _____

_____

In different spaces in your home, you may respond to different things. One color may help you focus in the office but feel stressful in the living room. As your life changes over time, you may want to repeat this exercise and reevaluate your space. Taking stock of the space around you can help you weed out unnecessary stressors and put supportive stimuli in place.

YOUR OPTIMAL LEVEL OF STIMULATION

HSP literature often uses the term *overarousal*, which can be confusing to those who do not experience high sensitivity. This book uses the term *overstimulation*, as it is descriptive of the biological process of stimulation to the central nervous system (CNS). In order to better understand overstimulation, let's start with a simplified overview of the CNS, which is made up of your brain and spinal cord. It is essential in things you register consciously (e.g., thoughts, movements, and emotions) and things that occur without your awareness (e.g., breathing, heart pumping, hormone regulation, and temperature regulation) (Newman, 2017). The CNS is where all five senses are processed, which is key to how an HSP experiences the world differently from a non-HSP. An international group of researchers reviewed the multiple functional MRI (fMRI) studies on HSPs that have been conducted to date. Consistently, the different brain structures measured showed up as more active in HSP populations than in non-HSP populations (Greven et al., 2019).

Everyone has limits to what their CNS can handle and can reach a point of feeling overwhelmed. For example, everyone has different ideal temperatures for working and feels too hot or too cold at varying rates, eventually hitting a temperature where they become sluggish, distracted, and/or unable to work in their normal fashion. The ideal temperature for an HSP might be much more specific than for a non-HSP. The heightened sensitivity of HSPs essentially means heightened processes of the CNS. While this carries benefits for HSPs (e.g., depth of understanding, empathic connection), it also means it is easier to hit limitations and experience distress and decreased functioning.

With any stimulus, the CNS of an HSP is processing at a deeper level than that of a non-HSP. This can be exhausting for HSPs, as the entire brain and spinal column are processing large amounts of data all the time. If you are running multiple complex processes on a computer, you might expect that its efficiency occasionally decreases. It can be the same for people when their brain structures are more active—think of HSPs as running more complex apps than non-HSPs. This is why you might pause before answering a question or need to wait until you are in a quiet office before responding to emails.

CONTINUED

Your CNS is constantly digesting data and then responding to help regulate your body. A regulatory response—for example, crying, which releases stress hormones like cortisol—is one that helps bring the CNS back into balance. Having a compassionate response toward yourself as your body works to find a regulated balance of CNS functioning can be helpful even if you cannot change the stimulus throwing it out of balance. Other CNS responses such as flushing (skin redness) and heart palpitations are your body's way of regulating overstimulation. Mindfulness practices can be crucial in learning how your CNS responds and giving space for self-regulating practices of the body.

Assessing Stimulation Levels

Understanding what stimulates you is helpful in creating a sustainable day-to-day rhythm. Take a minute to reflect on the following types of situations and write down examples that may be positive or negative for you. Keep in mind that the same stimulus might fit in both columns (e.g., meeting new people). When a stimulus might be good and bad, consider labeling the different pieces (e.g., coffee, in the table on page 19).

SOURCE OF STIMULATION	THINGS I LIKE	THINGS I DISLIKE
Physical: High-intensity sensory input (sight, taste, touch, sound, smell)	Ex: loud concert	Ex: car honking
Physical: Low-intensity sensory input (sight, taste, touch, sound, smell)	Ex: soft lighting	Ex: sound of HVAC unit

SOURCE OF STIMULATION	THINGS I LIKE	THINGS I DISLIKE
Cognitive: New experiences	Ex: adventure	Ex: uncertainty
Social: Being the center of attention	Ex: feeling included	Ex: fears of messing up
Physical: Substances (e.g., medications, sugar, caffeine)	Ex: coffee giving me energy	Ex: coffee giving me anxiety
Multidimensional: Surprises	Ex: romantic	Ex: overwhelming
Emotional: Emotional processing	Ex: sharing feelings with friends	Ex: watching a sad movie
Cognitive: Topics of deep discussion or thought	Ex: connecting with people	Ex: can feel heavy or sad

As you learn how different stimuli affect you, you can become more intentional about when and how you are exposed to certain stimuli (e.g., whether coffee would be helpful or hurtful in this moment). When you cannot control your exposure levels, try to understand why you feel overstimulated so that you can respond with self-compassion rather than self-blame. Simply understanding what is going on for you in a given moment can help calm anxiety.

COMMON CHALLENGES

It's challenging when an HSP cannot control the level of stimulation in the environment. You cannot control what lighting your employer uses, the music a store plays overhead, or the perfume a colleague wears. Sometimes just functioning in the world feels like an assault on your senses and leaves you feeling depleted, discouraged, and grumpy. You might then become snippy with a friend or loved one and subsequently feel guilt and shame.

Dealing with overstimulation is hard. To cope, use careful planning and preventive measures. Keep in mind that making decisions about the things within your control can also lead to overstimulation and decision fatigue, so pace yourself.

It's common and reasonable for HSPs to have periods of feeling attuned to how unfair and hard life can be for them. Wouldn't it be lovely to not need to plan ahead, have contingency plans, or worry about becoming overwhelmed? Unchecked, this can lead to self-shaming, or thinking that you should be more like other people and that being highly sensitive is "just in your head." This leads to a catch-22 where you may ignore your needs, leading to even more overstimulation, worsening your experience, and leaving you feeling even more different from other people.

Some days you will be in tune with the immense joy and beauty of being an HSP. Celebrate these! On days when you are in touch with how hard it can be, remember that the fantasy of not having limitations is just that—a fantasy. Everyone has limitations, and it is part of the human condition to face them and find a way to function. Everyone is born into a body and circumstances they did not choose. The work that must be done involves accepting the hand that was dealt and making the best of your situation. So feel the injustice, process the grief, give yourself space to work through it, and then begin finding where you have a sense of agency to improve what you can. Above all, remember that it's not "in your head"; it's in your central nervous system, which just happens to include your head.

Budgeting Resources

All tasks take time, physical energy, mental focus, and emotional bandwidth. You have limits to how many hours you can be productive in a given day. To manage your time is to manage these limited resources. Powering through and borrowing resources from your future will lead to overstimulation and burnout.

Knowing how much time you need to sleep and wake rested, to transition between tasks, to eat without rushing, etc. can help you set realistic goals in daily and weekly productivity. Abiding by your limitations can actually increase your effectiveness in each activity because you will be in your optimal range.

1. Below, list all of your needs and wants in your professional and personal lives for the next week. As you practice this inventory, you may wish to incorporate this exercise, or a variation of it, into your daily, weekly, or monthly planning routine.

	WORK/SCHOOL	PERSONAL
NECESSITIES	Ex: deadlines, requirements, meetings, classes	Ex: hygiene, food, sleep, doctor appts; include one self-care activity
WANTS	Ex: ongoing projects, tasks without deadlines	Ex: socializing, projects

2. Use the lists on page 21 to start creating a schedule. Take items from the lists and put them in blocks of time beginning on page 24.

   » First, put in your sleep, including routines around sleeping and waking.

   » Next, pull from your list of needs and begin plugging the tasks into the hour slots beginning on page 24, dividing each into 15- or 30-minute slots as necessary. If you use an electronic calendar, you can do this activity there.

   » Add the wants, knowing that some of these may get bumped depending on how many needs are competing for resources.

   » Account for *everything* (e.g., transportation times, break times, relaxation). It is common for your goals and expectations to exceed the amount of time available to achieve those goals. Something has to give. People often sacrifice sleep, nutrition, and self-care. This puts you on a crash course toward burnout, especially for HSPs.

PRO TIP: Include one or two blocks of buffer time each week for unexpected problems that might arise. This allows for controlled flexibility and can alleviate panic if you don't complete a task in the allotted time frame.

PRO TIP: Assess how long you can hold attention and focus without a break (could be 30 minutes, could be 4 hours), and set your expectations accordingly. The goal is to set yourself up for success with achievable expectations.

3. At the end of the week, come back to this exercise. Take a moment to reflect on the following before trying again the following week.

   » What worked well? _____

   _____

   _____

   _____

» Where did I need more time that I thought? _____

_____

_____

_____

» What can I change to improve my experience next week? _____

_____

_____

_____

» A common realization is that there is not enough time for everything. If this was true for you, are there areas where you can cut back? What needs to give?

_____

_____

_____

4. Keep revisiting and tweaking this exercise as you need until you find a sustainable schedule or method of scheduling that you can use week to week.

Budgeting your time to account for everything that needs to be done can be immensely helpful in managing anxiety and feelings of overwhelm. Having a reliable and functional calendaring system is a proactive way to budget your limited resources of time and energy.

SUNDAY

12 a.m.	12 p.m.
1 a.m.	1 p.m.
2 a.m.	2 p.m.
3 a.m.	3 p.m.
4 a.m.	4 p.m.
5 a.m.	5 p.m.
6 a.m.	6 p.m.
7 a.m.	7 p.m.
8 a.m.	8 p.m.
9 a.m.	9 p.m.
10 a.m.	10 p.m.
11 a.m.	11 p.m.

MONDAY

12 a.m.	12 p.m.
1 a.m.	1 p.m.
2 a.m.	2 p.m.
3 a.m.	3 p.m.
4 a.m.	4 p.m.
5 a.m.	5 p.m.
6 a.m.	6 p.m.
7 a.m.	7 p.m.
8 a.m.	8 p.m.
9 a.m.	9 p.m.
10 a.m.	10 p.m.
11 a.m.	11 p.m.

TUESDAY

12 a.m.	12 p.m.
1 a.m.	1 p.m.
2 a.m.	2 p.m.
3 a.m.	3 p.m.
4 a.m.	4 p.m.
5 a.m.	5 p.m.
6 a.m.	6 p.m.
7 a.m.	7 p.m.
8 a.m.	8 p.m.
9 a.m.	9 p.m.
10 a.m.	10 p.m.
11 a.m.	11 p.m.

WEDNESDAY

12 a.m.	12 p.m.
1 a.m.	1 p.m.
2 a.m.	2 p.m.
3 a.m.	3 p.m.
4 a.m.	4 p.m.
5 a.m.	5 p.m.
6 a.m.	6 p.m.
7 a.m.	7 p.m.
8 a.m.	8 p.m.
9 a.m.	9 p.m.
10 a.m.	10 p.m.
11 a.m.	11 p.m.

THURSDAY

12 a.m.	12 p.m.
1 a.m.	1 p.m.
2 a.m.	2 p.m.
3 a.m.	3 p.m.
4 a.m.	4 p.m.
5 a.m.	5 p.m.
6 a.m.	6 p.m.
7 a.m.	7 p.m.
8 a.m.	8 p.m.
9 a.m.	9 p.m.
10 a.m.	10 p.m.
11 a.m.	11 p.m.

12 a.m.	12 p.m.
1 a.m.	1 p.m.
2 a.m.	2 p.m.
3 a.m.	3 p.m.
4 a.m.	4 p.m.
5 a.m.	5 p.m.
6 a.m.	6 p.m.
7 a.m.	7 p.m.
8 a.m.	8 p.m.
9 a.m.	9 p.m.
10 a.m.	10 p.m.
11 a.m.	11 p.m.

SATURDAY

12 a.m.	12 p.m.
1 a.m.	1 p.m.
2 a.m.	2 p.m.
3 a.m.	3 p.m.
4 a.m.	4 p.m.
5 a.m.	5 p.m.
6 a.m.	6 p.m.
7 a.m.	7 p.m.
8 a.m.	8 p.m.
9 a.m.	9 p.m.
10 a.m.	10 p.m.
11 a.m.	11 p.m.

Automating Activities

Use this exercise repeatedly for any activities for which you would like a routine. Having a routine allows you to free up mental energy and increase efficiency in daily activities. Remember, it is better to overestimate time needed than to underestimate. Be generous in your planning to avoid feeling rushed in your routines.

How much time do I need for this routine? _____

_____

Transition time: How much time before or after this routine do I need for transitioning?

_____

List every task that needs to be accounted for in this routine. In parentheses after each task, put the estimated amount of time needed.

Example: Morning routine: 30 min: brush teeth (2 min), eat breakfast (15 min), meditate (5 min), get dressed (3 min), do hair (5 min)

_____

_____

_____

_____

_____

_____

_____

_____

Add up the times in the parentheses above. Are they equal to or less than your ideal time frame?

_____

_____

If they add up to more than your ideal time frame, either increase the amount of time for the whole activity or reduce the items you expect to accomplish.

Does the order matter?

_____

If so, in what order would you like to do these?

_____

_____

_____

_____

_____

_____

_____

As you are building this routine, post your finalized list somewhere visible. This reminder can be helpful to refocus or direct you until the routine is so familiar that the reminder is no longer necessary.

REFLECTING ON PAST EXPERIENCES

Growing up as an HSP can be incredibly hard and painful, depending on a multitude of contributing factors. Everyone is shaped by macrosystems, like your generation, gender, and culture, as well as microsystems, like your family, community, and classrooms. Depending on how others responded to your HSP nature, you may have thrived or struggled. These responses helped form the templates you use to evaluate yourself in relation to the world around you. For example, are you "weird," "eccentric," or "gifted" in your sensitivity?

Greven et al. (2019) remind us that HSP is a trait, not a disorder, and can have an interaction effect with positive and negative experiences. This means that the trait itself did not dictate the outcome of your childhood. But when HSPs have negative experiences, they are more susceptible to negative outcomes than non-HSPs, such as developing depression or anxiety or having poor health. Fortunately, it also means that when HSPs have positive experiences, they can have more positive outcomes than non-HSPs, such as higher levels of creativity or feelings of pleasure and meaning.

When evaluating your past, it can be helpful to keep this interaction effect in mind. It can give you space to recall the challenges you faced as an HSP as well as the contributions this trait made to your experiences. It can be easy to hear the research and feel doomed to a life of anxiety or depression because HSPs react strongly to their environment. Yet it is often the case that HSPs can recall a small gesture or comment from someone in their childhood that was incredibly calming or soothing and that continues to bring comfort in stressful times. When reflecting on your past, try to keep in mind both the positive and negative effects of being an HSP and how they can balance each other.

Processing Memories

Spending time reflecting on your past experiences can help bring clarity to present emotions. Recalling positive experiences can help ground you and balance negative thoughts about being an HSP.

Take a moment to recall and write about a positive *memory from childhood.*

_____

_____

_____

_____

_____

_____

_____

_____

_____

» How did your HSP traits enhance this experience?

_____

_____

_____

_____

» Who experienced this with you?

_____

_____

» How did their reactions contribute to your experience?

_____

_____

_____

_____

Now recall and write about a negative *memory from childhood.*

_____

_____

_____

_____

_____

_____

_____

_____

_____

_____

» How did your HSP traits worsen this experience?

_____

_____

_____

_____

» What people do you associate with this memory?

_____

_____

» How did their reactions contribute to your experience?

_____

_____

_____

_____

Future exercises will go more in depth with early life experiences, but this exercise serves to introduce balancing the concept of "both/and." Being an HSP is *both* hard *and* good. Holding this tension is essential to grieving and celebrating the reality of this trait.

Highly Sensitive People and Social Situations

Just like with environmental stimuli, you will have unique gifts and challenges in social contexts. When interacting with others, depth of processing occurs when observing non-verbal communication and listening to content, subtext, and context. With each additional person added to an interaction, you may experience exponential complexity in what you are processing. There can also be additional sources of contextual pressures (e.g., messages that you are being "too quiet"), environmental stimuli (e.g., multiple people talking at the same time), and nonverbal communication (e.g., noticing who is uncomfortable).

Let's say Dani (HSP) and Yuki (non-HSP) are colleagues who decide to grab lunch during the workday. Dani appreciates the lunch because Yuki is open to deep conversation and is comfortable with Dani occasionally being quiet. One day Yuki invites a new colleague, Marion, to lunch. Marion and Yuki are both pleasant and the conversation is good, yet Dani notices she is exhausted at the end of lunch. She feels disappointed and a bit confused. Marion is nice, Yuki is nice, they all laughed a lot, and both Marion and Yuki expressed excitement about the three of them doing this again sometime. Dani starts to wonder, "What's wrong with me? Marion and Yuki don't seem bothered by this. I think I'm just being too sensitive." The next day, Dani feels torn between needing rest during lunch and not wanting to miss out on the social activity.

When it's just her and Yuki, Dani is aware of their dynamic and attuned to how Yuki is reacting and experiencing things. She also has breaks where she can process her environment, the conversation, her food, etc. and not feel overwhelmed. When a dyad (Dani-Yuki) turns into a triad (Dani-Yuki-Marion), she moves from tracking one set of interactions in the dyad to four sets of interactions: (1) Dani-Yuki dyad, (2) Dani-Marion dyad, (3) Marion-Yuki dyad, and (4) Dani-Marion-Yuki triad. For each person added to a group, HSPs tend to be processing this exponential increase in data streams.

Additionally, HSPs often feel pressure to respond when they notice someone's discomfort. While this is a kind gesture, it is a gift and not a requirement. Some days you may feel up for talking to the anxious newcomer in the corner to help them feel included, and other days you may not.

Allow yourself permission to:

» Shift into more of an observer role in groups.

» Regularly check in with yourself and what you need.

» Remind yourself that it is not your responsibility to make sure everyone is perfectly comfortable.

» Say no.

» Arrive late or leave early.

» Take breaks.

» Change your mind.

» Treat yourself the way you would treat a friend.

In any social situation, you are navigating competing needs, such as the need for social inclusion and the need for manageable stimulation. Your needs are always in flux, so checking in with yourself and being flexible is important. For example, Dani may decide that sometimes she can go out to lunch with her colleagues, some days she may want to meet one-on-one, and some days she may want to eat by herself. Each decision comes with a loss (increased tiredness, someone feeling left out, or missing out socially, respectively) and Dani has to negotiate what level of loss feels workable for her.

Do I Go to This Event?

Follow this decision tree to help you decide whether you will attend an event based on what you value and what limited resources you have available for the event.

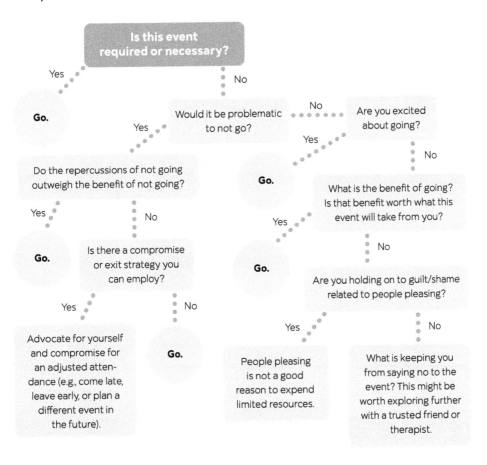

There will always be times when you have to attend an event that is draining for you, but assessing *why* and *how* to attend an event can help limit unnecessary drains on your resources. And by gaining more clarity about how you can balance your energy outputs and inputs, you can attend important events and be engaged while also being attuned to your personal needs.

Mindful Self-Check

So you have decided to attend an event that requires something of you socially. Mindfully preparing for the event and your aftercare can help preserve your resources. Use the list on page 36 to check in with yourself before, during, and after an event.

» What is my body telling me? How does this relate to my feelings about the event and the people there?

Example: When I get back from networking, I usually get a headache. I am probably holding the stress of meeting new people in my shoulders and neck. When I start to feel neck or head pain, it may be a good indication that I am stressed.

_____

_____

_____

_____

_____

» Do I feel drained or energized by the event/people?

_____

_____

» What do I need for this to feel successful?

Example: To feel content at the end of the event, I usually need to have one or two deep conversations.

_____

_____

_____

_____

» How much energy/resources do I currently have to give toward the event/people?

Example: I haven't been able to sleep enough this week due to a deadline at work, and I likely can't be energetic and upbeat during a four-hour event. I can either go and "be on" for an hour before going home, or I can be a laid-back participant for the full four hours.

_____

_____

_____

_____

_____

_____

» What do I need afterward for recovery?

Example: Extra sleep, an introvert day, extra hydration or health food, a hot bath, etc.

_____

_____

_____

_____

» What needs do I have that might be competing? Am I okay with the need that is currently winning and the cost I am paying to meet this need?

Example: I need nine hours of sleep to feel good for work. I also need social time with a friend I haven't seen in over a year. To stay up late talking with this friend means I will be tired at work for the next few days. Am I okay with that sacrifice?

_____

_____

_____

_____

_____

_____

_____

_____

» What can I plan in advance that would be helpful?

Example: I want to go hiking on Saturday, but that is usually when I do my laundry. I will stay home Friday night to do my laundry so that I can just rest when I am done hiking on Saturday.

_____

_____

_____

_____

_____

_____

_____

» How will I know when I have reached my limit?

Example: I start to feel tired, my feet hurt, and I don't follow stories as well when I start to feel overwhelmed. When I notice any one of these, that is a good indication that I am overstimulated and need to head home or take a break.

_____

_____

_____

_____

» When I feel ready to be done, what is my exit strategy?

Example: I will drive my own car so that when I feel ready to leave, I can go and not wait on someone else or force them to leave early. I've let the host know that I may need to leave early, and when I am ready I will say bye to these three people and head home.

_____

_____

_____

_____

» If I cannot leave early, what can help me sustain my energy?

Example: I will bring a snack and get a coffee, find a quiet corner where I can take a rest break, nap beforehand, and clear my morning schedule for tomorrow so I can sleep in.

_____

_____

_____

_____

Over time, these questions will become more ingrained and fluid for you as you assess giving your resources to different events and people. For now, it can be helpful to be intentional about checking in with yourself. The more data you have, the more informed decisions you can make moving forward.

COMMON CHALLENGES

HSPs are often so in tune with other people that it can be easy to ignore their own needs. Messages received early in life can reinforce this self-neglect, as can the belief that your sensitivity is invalid. People tend to respond positively when they feel cared for, so caring for others can be both rewarding and draining. A healthy goal for an HSP is giving at least equal voice to your needs as you do to other people's needs.

Finding a healthy balance in negotiating needs can be hard. HSPs don't get to decide everything just because they are sensitive, but they also don't need to "suck it up and deal with it" because no one else feels the same way. Balance cannot be found without open communication. Non-HSPs may not pick up on your discomfort in the way you pick up on the discomfort of others; therefore, explicit communication is important. Speak up by first sharing how you feel and then request an adjustment.

Self-advocacy often occurs in small ways, like a comment here or there. Speaking up does not mean everyone will give you what you want, but using your voice can boost your confidence, help you retain your sense of agency, and inform you about the type of people you are in relationships with. That is, if your friends make you feel bad for being sensitive, it might be a good time to expand your friend group.

REFLECTING ON PAST EXPERIENCES

The depth of processing that HSPs do, along with heightened emotional experience, means that negative experiences can get locked in. Early experiences create templates for how you experience things moving forward. These templates run automatically in the background (e.g., assuming someone is annoyed with you because your family was always annoyed when you brought up a sensitivity-related concern). HSPs are often familiar with feeling different and misunderstood. In groups, especially groups of children, being different is often associated with being isolated, teased, or embarrassed.

A common theme that comes up for adult HSPs is that they worked hard to not be a burden to their family and to take care of themselves as children. As children, HSPs often cope with negative experiences internally (they feel shame and adjust their behavior on their own) and don't share them with adult caretakers who might help reframe, process emotions, or intervene for the child. Highly sensitive children learn how to meet their own needs and parent themselves and are often praised for being "low maintenance." What gets missed is the hurt, scared, sad, or lonely experience of the highly sensitive child.

Having needs that were missed is not always indicative of poor parenting. Often people are born into families where the style of parenting is a poor fit for the personality and sensory processing needs of the child. Attending to the missed needs later in life does not necessitate condemning the caretaker. But knowing that you had certain needs that were not or could not be met can open the door for self-compassion. Building resiliency starts with understanding your past emotions and experiences.

Early Messages

Growing up as an HSP is often confusing and isolating, especially if this label is not discovered until adulthood. Reflecting on your past through the HSP lens can help you reframe negative experiences. Consider the questions that follow as you reflect. Know that these may be questions you want to digest one at a time, so feel free to return to this list as often as is helpful.

» What messages did you receive from authority figures (e.g., parents, other family members, teachers) around sensitivity?

What was communicated explicitly?

What did you pick up on implicitly (e.g., through observing nonverbal communication or indirect comments)?

_____

_____

_____

_____

_____

_____

_____

» What messages did you receive from peers around sensitivity?

  What was communicated explicitly?

  What did you pick up on implicitly?

_____

_____

_____

_____

_____

_____

_____

_____

» Did you understand your sensitivity as something to be valued, something to overcome, or something else?

_____

_____

» In what way, if any, did gender factor into messages you received around sensitivity?

_____

_____

_____

_____

_____

» In what way, if any, did race factor into messages you received around sensitivity?

_____

_____

_____

_____

_____

» In what way, if any, did faith or religion factor into messages you received around sensitivity?

_____

_____

_____

_____

_____

» What would have been helpful for you, as a child, in managing your sensitivity in different contexts (e.g., home environment, family dynamics, school expectations, socializing with peers, faith events)?

_____

_____

_____

_____

_____

_____

_____

» What challenges did you face due to being an HSP that you did not realize at the time?

_____

_____

_____

_____

_____

Reflecting on your past can be an intense experience. Allow yourself space to experience whatever emotions arise. Taking inventory of your past will help provide insight into why and how you respond to things now. It grants space for self-compassion and understanding that can move you toward growth and new experiences. This type of growth takes time, energy, and emotional resources.

CHAPTER RECAP

HSPs are constantly processing data from their environment and integrating that data with past and present experiences. This can cause feelings of overwhelm and exhaustion. Being mindful of this potential for overstimulation can help you create life rhythms that are more accommodating of your needs, thus allowing for more optimal functioning. As you continue to move through your daily routines, keep the following in mind:

1. There is a biological basis for your sensitivity, and anxiety/overwhelm is your CNS communicating that it needs attention.

2. Finding your optimal levels of stimulation will allow for more sustained energy and a sense of calm from day to day.

3. Reprocessing memories in light of the HSP label can give space for self-compassion and rewrite the narrative of your life in an empowering way.

CHAPTER THREE

Relationships

Relationships are hard. You may find yourself torn between the desire to connect and how hard it is to have authentic relationships. They are fraught with opportunities for misunderstanding, manipulation, and pain. And yet, a good relationship can increase quality of life, improve health outcomes (Yang et al., 2016), and enhance the joy of new experiences. Relationships are worth having, but they are also worth being selective about because they can help or hinder your life significantly. This chapter will touch on different types of relationships and navigating needs within each.

Highly Sensitive People in Romantic Relationships

Regardless of your current relationship status, remember that being in a long-term, committed relationship is not a healthy main goal in life. Many cultural messages point toward romantic relationships as essential to having meaning and purpose in life, yet this is not satisfying and fulfilling to everyone. For those who identify as asexual, prefer being single, or have yet to meet someone to whom they would like to commit, remember that self-worth is not dependent on romance. Take what is helpful from the discussion on page 63 regarding types of relationships and release yourself from the lie that you need someone else to make you whole. If you are in a romantic relationship, keep in mind that your wholeness exists outside of your partner. Practicing intentional communication, sharing responsibility and goals, and nurturing individual interests are all helpful relationship tools, especially for HSPs.

INTENTIONAL COMMUNICATION. Some HSPs fear their needs are too much for non-HSPs and wonder if they need to be in a relationship with another HSP. Others consider that having two HSPs in a relationship can be a lot to navigate. Both groups have legitimate concerns, and there is no "right" answer. For an HSP, it can be intimidating to label and ask for what you need. For a non-HSP, it can be hard to admit you also have needs and to express them when they seem less intense than the HSP's needs. For both groups, it can be helpful to identify the difference between wants and needs. A non-HSP may prefer a cool environment for sleep, but an HSP may be unable to sleep if it is too hot. What is a preference for one might be a need for another, and being able to communicate clearly about this is important. When you can identify and state your needs, listen compassionately to your partner's needs, and work together for compromise, it can create a profound experience of safety, compassion, and connection.

SHARED EXPERIENCE OVER COMPETITION. In romantic relationships, it is helpful to move out of a mind-set of competition, where you see yourself as "winning," "losing," or "getting your way." Consider moving into a mind-set of shared experience. The goal is for the couple, as a unit, to have their needs met and to enjoy themselves. If one person is suffering, then it is likely that the unit is suffering, and it can be helpful to intervene for the benefit of everyone. For example, non-HSPs may need to be reminded that topics cannot be consistently avoided simply because the HSP partner will be emotional. These emotions need space to be processed, and the HSP needs to know how to handle emotional fluctuations. HSPs can have big emotions *and* be okay, even better, after processing emotions effectively. This will likely take more time than it would for a non-HSP, and that's okay.

INTENTIONAL SOLO TIME. Not every activity needs to be done together. If Jordan loves going to loud concerts and Hyun loves quiet evenings in, it would make sense for this couple to schedule some activities apart. Being intentional about when they do things together versus apart is essential to Jordan and Hyun being on the same page. Identifying which activities are couple, friend, or solo activities can be helpful. Occasionally sharing things together, like Hyun going to a concert with Jordan or Jordan doing a puzzle with Hyun, is also important. Sharing why certain activities are important to you and understanding why your partner loves what they love goes a long way to limiting resentfulness, feeling seen and cared for by your partner, and helping your partner prioritize what they need to feel good. Respectful, intentional communication and mindful joint decision-making can lead to both partners' needs being accounted for.

Curating Good Experiences

When planning events, consider the feelings and needs of both you and your partner. You want to plan activities where both members can participate within their respective limitations. What does each person need so that the individuals and the couple unit can enjoy the day?

Ask your partner: What do you need during [activity] to feel like it is a good experience?

Ask yourself: What do I need to feel [activity] is a good experience?

After brainstorming these questions, follow this basic template.

1. Plan ahead

   » What health needs will you each have?

_____

_____

_____

_____

» What environmental needs will you each have?

_____

_____

_____

_____

» What emotional needs will you each have?

_____

_____

_____

_____

» When potential needs arise, what will be your contingency plan(s)? How will each partner respond in the event of these needs?

_____

_____

_____

_____

» What is the priority for each person?

_____

_____

_____

_____

2. Experience

   » Check in with yourself and your partner.

   » How is everyone doing? Are there needs that are arising?

   _____

   _____

   _____

   _____

   » If so, can you implement one of the contingency plans? Or can you problem-solve together if it is an unexpected need?

   _____

   _____

   _____

   _____

3. Debrief

   » What went well in this experience?

   _____

   _____

   _____

   _____

   » What would you like to do differently next time?

   _____

   _____

   _____

   _____

» Remember that failures will happen. Try to reflect on and address them without shaming the other person.

As with many exercises in this book, this will get easier over time. As you get used to checking in with yourself and your partner, you can begin to find comfortable rhythms that allow you to enjoy experiences more fully, which can also have the added benefit of bringing you and your partner closer together.

Communicating Effectively

The following exercise will be much easier if you and your partner have healthy patterns of communicating. As you and your partner discuss the exercise, practice the following:

» When you answer a question, have your partner reflect your response back to you, and you do the same for them. Not like a parrot, but in a way that ensures you understand what they are saying.

Example A: Partner 1: "I know one of my health needs is making sure I have a snack every two to three hours so I don't get grumpy or shaky." Partner 2: "Great. Let's make sure we pack enough so that you have food to eat when you need it and so that if I need a snack, I am not taking from what you need."

Practice: Using this passage as an example, think of something your partner recently shared with you about their needs and practice rewriting it in a reflective way:

_____

_____

_____

_____

PRO TIP: Use "I" statements when giving feedback, and practice reflecting back when you are receiving feedback.

Example B: Partner 2 ended up needing Partner 1's jacket. Upon debriefing, Partner 1 said, "When you needed my jacket, I felt angry because I had planned ahead for this. In the future, I would like for you to pack a jacket as well so that we can both have what we need." Partner 2: "I understand that you felt frustrated. I know I typically don't need a jacket. But in the future, I can carry my own to make sure we both have what we need."

Practice: Using this passage as an example, think about a piece of feedback you or your partner recently gave. Reword it here as an "I" statement:

_____

_____

_____

_____

_____

PRO TIP: Avoid name-calling, blaming, or bringing up the past.

Continuing with example B, the following are examples of poorly worded pieces of feedback from Partner 1 to Partner 2: "You are so selfish." "It's your fault I was cold all night." "This is just like that other time when you took my jacket."

PRO TIP: It's important to note here that many people, if not most, can fall prey to these negative types of interactions. For these exercises, try not to focus too much on your responses in the past, and think more about how you might be able to make small but important changes in your communication for the future.

Practice: Do you do any of these with your partner? If so, practice rephrasing an example using the skills highlighted in examples A and B.

_____

_____

_____

_____

_____

These can be hard strategies to learn. If you find yourself struggling in communication with your partner or have long-established unhealthy patterns, consider seeking the help of a couples therapist. If you are starting a new long-term, committed relationship, it can be helpful to proactively seek couples therapy to learn tools to prevent and cope with conflict effectively. Think of it like seeking a personal trainer at the beginning of getting into exercise, so you can learn proper form before you build your exercise regimen, rather than seeking help much later after injury occurs. Therapy can be both preventive and reactive.

COMMON CHALLENGES

It is easy to become angry and defensive in difficult conversations. Remind each other that you care about each other and are seeking understanding so that each of you can have a positive experience. You may think "this is obvious," but it can calm anxiety substantially when someone you care about makes this explicit in a difficult conversation. It is important for both partners to create a safe space to share, process, and problem-solve.

For non-HSPs in relationships with HSPs, it can be difficult or draining to constantly be "processing" information. Making the processing of negative emotions or experiences intentional and contained by activity or time can help (e.g., in the hour after you get home from work or while on a walk). Afterward, try making a conscious effort to shift focus to positive conversation topics or gratitude exercises in order to help balance the draining effect of processing negative experiences.

When processing negative experiences for HSPs, ask them what would be helpful. Do they need validation? Understanding? Solutions? When in doubt, ask. The HSP may not know what they need but, by asking, you show that you care and are invested in helping. As the HSP in the relationship, proactively share your needs. While it is nice to have someone anticipate your needs, your partner won't know what you need, so learning to speak up will help both of you. Remember to reciprocate these questions and considerations to make sure there is space for the needs of both partners.

HSPs sometimes need to process negative experiences repeatedly, which can be hard for non-HSPs, who might be tempted to say things like "I thought we already discussed this." Learning how to discuss differences in a nonshaming manner is important. While an HSP may have more needs, this does not mean they take precedence. You would not get mad at your partner (hopefully) if they had a seafood allergy. You would find restaurants where they could eat safely. When you want fish, you would make arrangements to go with a friend and communicate this with your partner. As the person with the allergy, it is helpful to express appreciation when your partner finds safe restaurants and to understand when they want to go get fish with a friend. Clear communication and compromise will come up time and again as crucial building blocks for relationships.

Managing Guilt and Shame

HSPs often limit how much they share due to feeling guilt, shame, or embarrassment around their emotional reactions and needs. This often relates to previous experiences of being told they are too sensitive or overreacting. Creating a safe space for sharing and limiting judgment is important in developing a deeper connection.

What emotions keep you from sharing concerns with your partner?

☐ Feeling like a burden

☐ Fear of abandonment

☐ Anger around your own limits

☐ Feeling weak

☐ Wanting to fit in

☐ Fear of rejection

☐ Fear of being teased

☐ Recalling a painful memory

☐ Overwhelm preventing you from thinking clearly

☐ Distracted from listening to your body (e.g., having too much fun)

☐ Other: _____

Are these feelings that you can share with your partner? Why or why not?

_____

_____

_____

_____

If you find yourself frequently avoiding vulnerability in your relationship, reflect on why this is. Trouble connecting with others, being vulnerable, or tolerating difficult conversations are indications that therapy could be helpful. Alternatively, consider whether this relationship is working for you if you cannot be fully present and vulnerable with your partner. Finally, remember that your partner is not your family of origin and that you have an opportunity to create new templates from the ones you developed growing up. It may take time and slow, repeated efforts toward vulnerability to start building healthy experiences and to create new relational patterns. Both you and your partner will be adapting and adjusting to new ways of connecting and communicating.

Asking for Help

Self-advocacy involves learning how to ask for help and acknowledging your own limits. In relationships it can be easy to frame your needs not being met as a failure of your partner. Practice taking these problematic statements and reworking them to be less shaming and more collaborative. Start with an "I" statement (*How do I feel?*), state your needs, then finish with a proposed way you can work together.

EXAMPLE

HSP feeling: Being overwhelmed by the actions of another.

Example of a problematic statement: "I need you to stop talking right now. You are overwhelming me."

» "I" statement that reduces shame and increases collaboration with the other person: "*I feel overwhelmed right now. I need a minute to collect my thoughts so that I can discuss this in a meaningful way and be helpful.*"

PRACTICE

Problematic statement: "I need the house to be cleaner, and I have already cleaned my stuff up."

» *Reword:* _____

_____

_____

Problematic statement: "I need the house to myself once a week. Can you leave every Saturday evening?"

» *Reword:* _____

_____

_____

Problematic statement: "I need us to stop eating junk food every day. It's bad for us."

» *Reword:* _____

_____

_____

Problematic statement: Think of an example of a term or phrase you use regularly with your partner that has room for improvement:

» *Reword:* _____

_____

_____

Collaboration helps move you away from a competitive win-lose dynamic where each partner is fighting for power. Instead, move toward a teamwork approach that prioritizes both of you and creates a safe and supportive connection. Working on how you phrase things in moments of vulnerability can go a long way in setting the tone for the relationship overall and building trust and safety with your partner.

REFLECTING ON PAST EXPERIENCES

What you learn in childhood becomes the template you use to understand the world, whether it is communication patterns, a sense of self-worth, or relational expectations. HSPs may see their past as an example of what *not* to do in relationships, but a template for healthy relationships remains vague and unclear. Whether your parents were high conflict or never fought in front of you, you might associate conflict with unhealthy relationships. Avoiding conflict can lead to HSPs minimizing their own needs, placating others, or seeking the path of least resistance in relationships in order to keep them "healthy." Possible effects of conflict avoidance are depression, resentment, low self-esteem, and feeling isolated.

You are not your parents, and you are not destined to have the same relationships they did. Your parents may have bickered a lot, which can be stressful for an HSP child, so you interpreted this type of conflict as bad. Yet your parents might be people who liked quick, direct feedback, spoke their minds, and then let things go. Alternatively, they may have never fought in front of you and had a very cold and distant relationship. Long story short—there are lots of varieties of healthy and unhealthy relationships. So seeing your parents in relationship with each other and/or other partners is helpful to reflect on—not to judge them but to think about what would work for you in your relationships. To be clear, physical violence is never an acceptable form of conflict in relationships. If this is currently affecting you or has previously affected you directly or indirectly, please seek help.

Giving and Receiving Feedback

It is unlikely you were given a choice in how your parents communicated with you or disciplined you. HSPs will often internalize that they cannot have a say in how people speak to them. This can lead to avoiding feedback altogether or suffering through unhealthy communication because they don't know any differently. Explore the following questions for yourself and your partner:

» Do you prefer in-the-moment feedback or scheduled feedback?

» How direct do you like the feedback to be? Succinct, short correction, or an Oreo-cookie-type correction (i.e., highlight something good, provide correction, reiterate something good)?

_____

_____

» How did your parents or caretakers give feedback when you were growing up?

_____

_____

_____

_____

» Are there phrases that would be helpful to avoid or change based on past experiences?

_____

_____

_____

_____

_____

» What do you need from your partner so you feel heard and understood?

_____

_____

_____

_____

_____

» How can you agree to disagree on certain topics?

Ask yourself if being right is necessary. That is:

Does someone's safety depend on it?
Is it a form of gaslighting (manipulative communication designed to make someone doubt their memory or perception)?
Will it significantly change the outcome of something?
Is it a battle worth fighting?

_____

_____

_____

_____

If not, would you rather be right or kind in this moment? Can you have different understandings of something and still hold compassion for each other?

_____

_____

_____

_____

Knowing what works for you and what doesn't helps you advocate for yourself and shape a culture of honest feedback that helps you grow. Being intentional and mindful around these processes builds a sense of agency for you, trust in the relationship, and the ability to adapt.

Identifying Expectations

It is helpful to explore how expectations are formed around romantic relationships. Consider how the following have influenced what you expect from your partner and what type of partner you expect yourself to be. Additionally, consider how gender, sexual identity, and sexual expression are handled by each of these.

» Media (movies, TV shows, songs, pop culture)

» Faith communities

» Family of origin

» Extended family

» Peers' families

» School/education

» Where you were raised (country, rural vs. urban environment)

Now consider how this has changed since you were a child (if you grew up in the 1960s, these topics were handled much differently than if you grew up in the early 2000s). What beliefs or expectations have changed for you over time?

_____

_____

_____

_____

_____

Again, knowing the whys of how you function can help you intentionally choose what works for you and what you would like to change. It can help you incorporate old and new practices that are congruent with your current values and goals in life. Taking stock of your influences helps you make informed decisions moving forward.

Highly Sensitive People
in Familial Relationships

It is not uncommon for anyone, HSP or non-HSP, to end up in a family where they feel different from everyone else. Whether you are an introvert born into a very social family or an artist born into a scientific family, it is common to feel out of place in your family of origin. The growth point, then, comes as you distinguish how you can connect with your family and when you need to set boundaries to take care of yourself. Boundaries are general rules around what you need to feel comfortable while interacting with another person.

SETTING BOUNDARIES. This involves defining your limits and values, being able to communicate them to others, and being able to respond in a healthy manner when others do not respect your boundaries. Boundaries exist on a spectrum with *porous* boundaries at one end (leading to burnout and resentment), *rigid* boundaries at the other (leading to loneliness and disconnection), and an ideal middle of *clear* boundaries for adult relationships. You will find your boundaries shift depending on the relationship and sense of safety you feel with the other person.

When Fu's family discusses politics, her stomach turns to knots and her adrenaline kicks into high gear. What her family considers "lively debate," Fu experiences as combative and hurtful. Fu began asking her family to not discuss politics around her and shared that if they would like to discuss this topic, she will step out of the room. This is an example of knowing what is unhelpful, communicating it, and having consequences for the behavior. You cannot prevent people from making their own choices (they will still talk about politics), but you can communicate clearly about how their choices affect you and then make your own choices around what is healthy for you.

DIFFERING BOUNDARIES. Your limits and the limits of your family members are going to be different. Your siblings might find these "lively debates" a meaningful way of connecting and experiencing life with family members. This is why learning about and understanding the other person is helpful. Be curious about each other; you do not have to agree or be the same in order to love and respect each other. This can make it easier to hold your own boundaries as well. For example, when family members begin discussing politics, Fu can wish everyone a happy debate and excuse herself to go for a walk, head to bed early, or invite nondebaters to play a board game in the other room. This can be a way to be nonshaming, nonblaming, and noncontrolling and respect her boundaries.

If you have siblings, you may find that you perceive and experience your parent(s) differently. What was encouraging and uplifting to one child may seem overbearing and obnoxious to another. As a parent, this can be discouraging because there is no way to be all things to all children. Adapt where you can, and be gracious to yourself and your child where you can't.

Identifying Boundaries

Boundaries will vary for you based on context and person, but having an understanding of boundary types can help you begin to communicate and implement them. Boundaries may be *rigid*, *clear*, or *porous*. Practice evaluating and labeling these different types of boundaries as R, C, or P, respectively.

RIGID: Hard, firm rules that may serve to limit intimacy, prioritize safety, prevent rejection, or devalue others. These do not take other people into consideration and can be experienced as arbitrary, detached, or distant by other people.

CLEAR: Clear understanding of your own needs or wants while being able to understand the needs or wants of others. You are comfortable saying no to others and being assertive when you need to.

POROUS: Overshare personal information, trouble saying no to others, devalue your own needs, overprioritize the needs of others, take responsibility for the emotions of others, passive to abuse or disrespect, strong fear of rejection or abandonment.

_____ A colleague states that people who believe in religion are stupid and do not belong in politics. He refuses to listen to other viewpoints.

_____ You go on a first date, and the other person talks about multiple traumas from their past, asks for your help in processing the traumas, and becomes angry when you change the subject.

_____ On a second date, you and the other person share what level of physical intimacy you are each comfortable with and expectations moving forward.

_____ A new neighbor knocks on your door and asks to use your car, informing you that if you don't help, their child will be stuck at school and their teachers will be angry.

_____ Your boss informs you that she is "a hugger" and expects that all employees give hugs as a greeting.

_____ You let your partner know you are up for a 20-minute walk and if they want additional exercise, they are welcome to continue without you.

After labeling these scenarios, ask yourself which situations feel uncomfortable. Can you label why they feel uncomfortable and what boundary each may be crossing for you?

_____

_____

_____

_____

_____

_____

COMMON CHALLENGES

One of the most common challenges for HSPs within their families is setting boundaries. It is difficult to change an established family system. People dislike when someone alters their ecosystem. This can feed into a family narrative that the HSP is being difficult, demanding, or too sensitive. Whenever anyone begins implementing boundaries, there will be a ripple effect. Remember Fu's realization that she does not do well with political debate? It is likely that her family will initially feel offended, defensive, or annoyed when Fu speaks up. They may make snarky comments like, "Oh, sorry, Fu. I *mentioned* the president. Is that allowed?" It is hard to implement change, and it will be imperfect as you move through it. Having the support of a therapist or friend who is adept at setting and communicating boundaries can be incredibly helpful.

Another challenge is deciding which events might be worth compromising for so that you can be a part of a family event while still honoring your limits. This might include renting a vacation house for the whole family to stay in together because you cannot afford to go on the trip *and* pay for your own lodging. Sometimes the ideal solution is not manageable. When this is the case, set contingency plans (e.g., going to coffee shops or taking naps), limit the amount of time you go (e.g., three days of a weeklong trip), and find healthy outlets (e.g., texting a supportive friend).

Labeling Your Boundaries

Roles and boundaries in your family of origin will change as people age. When families get together as adults, it is common to feel pulled back to the roles and boundaries from when you were younger. It can help to be intentional about how you want and need to interact with your family as you grow.

Thinking specifically about your family now, consider what boundaries you need. You can repeat this exercise for different contexts and people as needed. List your needs around:

Time: _____

_____

_____

_____

Emotions: _____

_____

_____

_____

Energy: _____

_____

_____

_____

Ideas/Beliefs: _____

_____

_____

_____

Money/Objects: _____

_____

_____

_____

It is hard to advocate for needs that you have not labeled. Identifying and communicating these needs with yourself can help you be prepared to communicate them with others. It can also help you understand when you feel distress because a boundary has been crossed.

Boundary Challenges

Anticipating challenges can help you not get caught off guard when you see your family next. Take some time to think about upcoming family interactions. Where can you anticipate conflict around your boundaries? And how do you want to try handling it this time? Keep in mind that cultural factors play a significant role in expectations and may need to be navigated differently depending on context.

With whom do you struggle to set boundaries?

_____

_____

What makes it difficult with this person?

_____

_____

_____

_____

What fears hold you back from saying no or being assertive?

_____

_____

_____

_____

What boundaries do you have that feel violated?

_____

_____

_____

_____

What actions can you take to begin making change?

_____

_____

_____

_____

Reflecting on these questions can help you identify whether or how to express your concerns to others. Resolving conflict can be much harder if you struggle to label what the conflict is, how it upsets you, or what needs to be done. You will not always be able to get what you want from your family, but having the insight around why you feel a certain way can help you regulate emotional responses (e.g., anger, hurt, anxiety) and support the need for self-care during or after the interactions.

REFLECTING ON PAST EXPERIENCES

For HSPs who grew up in families that did not understand the trait, there can be a long history of unintentional wounding. Many HSPs will have examples of emotional or sensory overwhelm, confusion, or hurtful comments from family members. Processing this history can be difficult, as the adult HSP feels torn between two realities: Either there is something wrong with the HSP, or their family (hopefully unintentionally) failed them and they must grieve the loss of the family they wish they had.

BAD FIT FRAMING. HSPs often default to blaming themselves for negative past experiences, as this maintains a sense of control. It gives the illusion that if they can "fix" themselves, they can have the relationship with their family that they always wanted. The idea of grieving a family that was not abusive, provided for basic needs, and all seemed to like one another can be a foreign concept. Implementing the framing of "bad fit" can be a nonblaming understanding of why the HSP has a hard time fitting in with the rest of the family.

FAMILY OF CHOICE. As one begins to grieve what they wish they had, they may benefit from identifying their "family of choice." This is contrasted with "family of origin," which no one can choose. *Family of choice* is an empowering term born out of the LGBTQ and recovery communities. One's family of origin may not have been the supportive environment that many assume when they use the term *family*, and these individuals knew how it felt to be rejected by their families of origin. This term has spread and is now used by many communities who feel a sense of loss and missed expectations regarding their families of origin. Building a supportive community who can understand, value, and respect your boundaries and needs can be an empowering way to meet the needs that your family of origin cannot or will not.

Building Your Family of Choice

Processing the missed expectations of childhood is exhausting, hard work. You can benefit from balancing it with gratefulness practices. Take a moment to inventory the positive influences in your life and the people who, in big or small ways, help you feel seen, valued, and understood. Keep in mind that your family of choice may include people from your family of origin.

Who is someone who . . .

» . . . notices when you are uncomfortable and offers words or gestures of comfort?

_____

» . . . lets you experience emotion without shame or blame?

_____

» . . . encourages you to take care of yourself?

_____

» . . . has complimented a strength you have from being an HSP?

_____

» . . . you can contact when you are having a hard time?

_____

Expanding your support system outside of your family of origin increases your ability to get your needs met. It is also an opportunity for you to celebrate joy and connection of all kinds.

PARENTING

Please note that a comprehensive consideration of child development and parenting approaches is beyond the scope of this book. Consider additional reading, such as The Highly Sensitive Child *(Aron, 2002).*

Being a parent means making sacrifices to ensure that your child is loved, cared for, and healthy. Your boundaries separating yourself from your child will, by necessity, be much more porous in the first years of life and become more defined as your child grows. As a parent, you are teaching your child how to meet their own needs while considering others, an essential skill set to function effectively in society. Teaching happens through your wins and losses; demonstrating how to tolerate failure and keep going is a crucial lesson for your child.

But how you teach boundaries and model engagement with the world will change as your child goes through developmental stages. At each stage, you have an opportunity to (a) provide containment and support for difficult emotions and (b) model healthy coping and communication. Regardless of age, remind your child that it is okay to have emotions; build a sense of safety, consistency, and stability; listen compassionately to their feelings; and empower them to decide how they want to handle their experiences. If you have children, you know by now that this is much easier said than done, so plan self-care and practice self-compassion.

Below you'll find some considerations around parent-child pairings to help guide your thinking with your own child. Consider these pairings in conjunction with the information in the chart on pages 73 and 74 as you explore how to support your child.

HSP Parent with Non-HSP Child. Your child may crave more stimulation and activity than you can provide comfortably. You may find yourself frequently overwhelmed and even angry at or annoyed with your child. Consider ways you can meet your child's needs through other means (e.g., signing up for extracurricular activities). Invite them into the process by asking them what they need and helping them problem-solve for how to meet those needs.

Non-HSP Parent with HSP Child. You may find yourself easily frustrated with how much your child is affected by the world. HSP children are both fragile and incredibly resilient. You cannot prevent them from having difficult emotions, but you can help them find ways to process, adapt to, and manage the emotions. Some might say, "Well, the world is a hard place, so I can't coddle them." True—avoiding distress will not teach them to cope with a difficult world. But throwing them into distress without coping tools, compassion, and validation will cause unnecessary distress and inhibit development.

HSP Parent with HSP Child. You will likely see yourself in your child, which may bring a mixture of pride, joy, anxiety, confusion, and sadness. Anxiety may be experienced, assuming that your child will struggle and internalize negative experiences in the same way you did. Remember, your child will have their own experiences. Checking in with them frequently and not assuming you know what they are feeling is important in allowing them space to grow into their own person.

	INFANCY TO PRE-K	ELEMENTARY	MIDDLE TO HIGH
PARENTING GOALS	» Help child explore environments » Modulate safety—the world is both scary and safe; communicating only one side of the spectrum is unhelpful	» Teach awareness of others » Develop learning skills and sense of productivity	» Develop moral and ethical reasoning—help them learn *how* to think rather than *what* » Help manage complex social dynamics » Teach ways to tolerate complex emotions
HSP CONSIDERATIONS	» Will likely be observant and quiet when entering new situations » May cry or throw tantrums when overstimulated » Empathy and emotional mirroring are important in learning emotional regulation and validation	» May be curious about the *why* of decisions » May benefit from explicit questions about their thoughts and feelings » May need help balancing awareness of self and others	» Preparing for adulthood may be overwhelming » May not realize what stress is or how it feels » May be particularly wounded by friendship/relationship ruptures

CONTINUED

	INFANCY TO PRE-K	ELEMENTARY	MIDDLE TO HIGH
INTERVENTIONS	» Help child identify and label what they like/dislike » Help identify and label emotions » Deep breathing exercises » Gentle stretching or movement » Taking breaks when overwhelmed » Build routines » Teach agency over one's body and ability to choose sensory input—allow them to say "no" to sensory input or social experience » Check in with them often about how they are doing » Use a 0 to 10 scale to rate emotions and experiences	» Build time for quiet play (puzzles, books, coloring), and loud play (parks, sports, board games) » Communicate with teachers around needing space to adjust/observe before participating » Structured family time for sharing » Conversations about negotiating competing needs from different people » Identify and support learning needs (e.g., tactile, visual, auditory) » Prepare them for new experiences by talking through environment and social dynamics » Create a calm, low-sensory-input workspace for them at home	» Talk through future goals and fears » Build support networks (mentors, teachers, extended family, religious leaders) » Identify markers of stress and what stress feels like in the body » Discuss and model self-care for stress management » Connect with extra-curricular activities » Brainstorm choices without dictating behavior » Allow child to experience failure and provide support through it » Talk about complex emotions, coping strategies, and frustration tolerance to try again and learn from mistakes

Shaping Expectations for Children

Children benefit from structure, predictability, and being able to understand the world around them. This all takes time and energy and can be hard for parents, especially those working multiple jobs. Adapting the exercise from earlier in this chapter, Curating Good Experiences (page 51), consider how planning, experiencing, and debriefing with your HSP child may help improve their (and your) ability to function in the world. The younger the child, the more modeling you will be doing until they develop the cognitive skills to be more interactive in the process. This is a trial-and-error process; each time you do this exercise you will learn something new. Your child will benefit from your efforts, and you will be modeling resiliency as you continue to try new things for better coping.

Highly Sensitive People in Friendships

HSPs can make good friends. They are often mindful of others, check in on people they haven't heard from in a while, and ask about emotional experiences. HSPs tend to be accommodating and can hold deep, meaningful conversations, which can be a breath of fresh air. That being said, HSPs may expect non-HSP friends to do the same. This can lead to feeling disappointed and resentful of friends who do not reciprocate this level of attentiveness. Adjusting expectations is essential for maintaining friendships.

If professional basketball player Steph Curry goes to a pickup basketball game at a local park and expects everyone to be able to play at the level of NBA players, he is going to be disappointed. He might even feel angry—why don't the other players just try harder? HSPs have heightened central nervous systems and emotional awareness skills. No matter how much non-HSPs "just try harder," it will not mean they can do what you can do. What feels obvious, basic, or common sense to you, may not even register for a non-HSP. Being aware that this is a strength does not make you arrogant, but how you talk about it in comparison to others might. Is Steph Curry arrogant if he acknowledges he is a good basketball player? No. But if he needs to repeatedly remind people how amazing he is and how inferior they are, it will lead to interpersonal problems.

Your friendship is a limited resource, a precious one, which has to be parsed out carefully. It can be life-giving to show up for people in times of need, to provide care, and to give to others what you wish someone would give to you. But giving indiscriminately and having porous boundaries will lead to burnout, resentment, and anger. In long-term friendships or relationships of any kind, there will be times when things are not fair. The goal is not a one-for-one exchange but an awareness of healthy reciprocity, feeling respected, and being able to ask for help.

Finding people with whom you can discuss differences and have healthy boundaries is the goal. As is being mindful of which friends can meet different needs. Culture often communicates that you should have one best friend with whom you do everything (similar to soul mate messages for romantic relationships). But this unrealistic expectation will lead inevitably to disappointment and hurt.

Friendship Superpowers

HSPs often devalue what they bring to relationships. Take a moment to reflect on the type of friend you are and what you bring to your friendships by checking off which friendship superpowers you have.

☐ Empathic to the emotions of others

☐ Loyalty that makes for good long-term friendships

☐ Willing to work through conflict

☐ Good sounding board for talking through difficult decisions—can hold a friend's values and needs in mind when considering choices

☐ Ability to read nonverbals and respond accordingly

☐ Empathy allows for quick reaction and accommodation when you notice that others are uncomfortable or have unmet needs

☐ Willing to engage deeply and talk about serious topics

☐ Less likely to be flippant or dismissive (e.g., being on your phone when out with a friend)

☐ Awareness of environmental stimuli and needs of self and others means you can plan comfortable and enjoyable experiences

☐ Other: _____

It can be easy as an HSP to be overly attuned to the ways you take up space in relationships and to minimize your contributions. Taking time to identify what you bring to a friendship can be helpful for your self-esteem and confidence.

COMMON CHALLENGES

In new friendships, it can be important to pace how much you give. People are drawn to HSPs because talking to you likely makes them feel good. This can be lovely, intoxicating, and validating—a new friend! Then, this person starts ghosting. The HSP combs their memory to find what went wrong. This is a common experience for HSPs and supports the misguided narrative that there is something "wrong" with the HSP. Being friends with an HSP can be challenging for a non-HSP because there is an expectation for genuine connection. HSPs may ask to work through conflict rather than ignoring it, ask for help when they feel overwhelmed, and live out their values. HSPs will express concern if a friend seems to be abandoning their values just to fit in. Non-HSPs can find this difficult and exhausting, and it is not uncommon for them to decide "this is too much, I'm out." Ouch.

Then come the negative thoughts: "if I could just let things go" or "if I could just be less sensitive." It is so painful. Please remember, if someone wants to be your friend, they will be open to you having needs. Whether it is friendship, family, or romantic connection, it is not your fault if the other person does not want to put in the work necessary to have a healthy relationship. You can grieve this loss without taking on shame. Shame is functional when it moves you toward treating others better and repairing a rupture in a relationship. But for this to happen, the other person needs to be openly sharing their feelings and invested in repairing the relationship.

Taking Inventory of Your Expectations

Negative emotions in relationships can often result from missed expectations. Identifying the expectations and how they were missed is the first step to addressing the concern and moving forward in the relationship.

Reflect on the relationships where you might feel some resentment, disappointment, or upset. Can you identify the expectation that is being missed?

_____

_____

_____

_____

Is the expectation unreasonable for this person's skill set?

_____

» If yes, how can you shift what you expect from the relationship? How do your boundaries need to shift to protect yourself?

_____

_____

_____

_____

» If no, is there a way you can discuss your concerns with them and work through the conflict? Remember that you cannot expect others to read your mind, no matter how obvious it may seem.

_____

_____

_____

_____

If you don't like conflict, it can be easy to avoid addressing feelings of hurt or anger in a relationship. In the long term, however, it means the relationship is no longer one you can enjoy and feel connected to. This can lead to a shallow support network where your needs and concerns are not addressed. While addressing conflict is hard, it is the path through which deep connections are forged.

Limiting Beliefs Checklist

HSPs may let past negative experiences limit their ability to connect with others in a healthy manner. What beliefs might be holding you back from healthy relationships?

☐ If I express my needs, others will see me as a burden.

☐ If I say no, others might reject or abandon me.

☐ If I speak up when someone hurts my feelings, they will dismiss or minimize me.

☐ I should be happy with the friends I have. At least I have someone I can do things with.

☐ I can find friends only by ignoring my needs and going along with what they want.

☐ Others: _____

These beliefs may be based on unhealthy previous experiences. Alternatively, they may be unrealistic fears that are holding you back from more meaningful friendships. Either way, a therapist or CBT workbook can help you work through these limiting beliefs.

REFLECTING ON PAST EXPERIENCES

Most people can recall childhood experiences of being made fun of, being excluded, or feeling different. For an HSP, these memories can become solidified as truths and shape their social identity. You may have already thought of a childhood memory that still makes you cringe. Your heightened emotional processing and ability for empathy means you can still feel some of the intense emotion that this experience caused. Ideally, you had a parent or trusted adult who helped you process and frame these experiences. If not, many HSPs benefit from processing these past emotions in therapy and finding new ways to frame those memories. Your current boundary needs will be shaped by these past experiences, especially if you can recall friendships where the emotions of others became overwhelming to you.

Reframing the Past

Finding new ways to frame and understand past experiences is a useful coping tool. Think of three past experiences around friendship that were painful or distressing in some way. Identify how each experience shaped your view of yourself, and consider a way to reframe it that empowers you moving forward.

Example:

EVENT: *NOT INVITED TO JESSE'S PARTY*
Limiting self-belief: *No one wanted to be my friend.*
Empowering reframe: *I would not have enjoyed that party anyway.*

4. Event: _____

   _____

   » Limiting self-belief: _____

   _____

   _____

   » Empowering reframe: _____

   _____

   _____

5. Event: _____

   _____

   » Limiting self-belief: _____

   _____

   _____

   » Empowering reframe: _____

   _____

   _____

6. Event: _____

_____

» Limiting self-belief: _____

_____

_____

» Empowering reframe: _____

_____

_____

The way you frame your reality matters. If you consistently believe that no one wants to be around you, being alone becomes a depressing experience. If you instead believe that time alone allows you to be a better friend when you are out, then you can value the time by yourself in a nonshaming way. Identifying and reframing these beliefs can go a long way in boosting your mental health.

Knowing Yourself in Friendships

Reflecting on the past is a great way to learn about yourself and move toward improved self-understanding and quality of life. Think specifically about friendships (good and bad) and social experiences—what do you need? Here are some questions to get you started:

» What is your ideal way to spend time with friends?

_____

_____

» How long can you spend with a friend and feel fully present?

_____

_____

» What boundaries do you need to limit absorbing their emotions?

_____

_____

» What is your preferred communication style with friends?

_____

_____

» How do you know when a friendship no longer works for you?

_____

_____

Thinking through what is and is not working in your friendships is a similar practice to the environmental assessments from chapter 2. Clearing away the clutter, finding what works, and implementing new strategies allows you to have a more positive experience of friendships and to be a better version of yourself when interacting with your friends.

CHAPTER RECAP

For every relationship in your life, think about ways to balance the needs of each person involved. Prioritizing communication, taking a stance of curiosity, and engaging in nonshaming problem-solving are helpful ways of maintaining healthy boundaries in relationships. Remember:

1. Boundaries may shift based on context, person, and your needs in a given moment. You and others are allowed to adjust boundaries as needed.

2. Use the mindfulness practice of planning, experiencing, and debriefing for yourself and others to have more enjoyable experiences.

3. Identifying differences does not have to result in judgment but can be a building block to open, honest communication.

CHAPTER FOUR

Work

Work can be a constant source of tension between conflicting needs for an HSP. On one hand there is a need to create a calm, ideally stimulating life, and on the other hand there is a need to make money to survive. Negotiating between these needs may take different forms over the course of your life. Being mindful of this ever-evolving process can help you make informed, intentional choices that move you toward your goals. In this chapter, you will begin to label the strengths you bring to your job and ways to leverage those in the workplace. Additionally, you will assess pain points in your work and ways to address or cope with them.

Highly Sensitive People and Vocation

How you frame your employment has an impact on your level of engagement with the work. HSPs often crave more than "just a job." A *job* serves as a means to an end—an exchange of your efforts for a paycheck. A *career* serves the purpose of advancement within a particular field. When working on your career, you are motivated toward growth, learning, and future opportunities. A *vocation* (or *calling*) combines a career with your moral and ethical values and is driven by connection to something outside of yourself. Examples of vocation include helping professions, faith-based positions, environmental protection, advocacy, and the like. In thinking about whether you want a job, career, or vocation, start by assessing your values.

Values Assessment

Consider the following list of values. This list is not exhaustive but includes common values people consider when making work-related decisions. Keep in mind that choosing a vocation, career, or job is a privileged position. If you are in a position right now where you do not have a choice in your employment, consider these in terms of future options or goals, your current work role, or nonwork commitments. Place an X on the line to indicate how influential each value is in work considerations.

Achievement/Accomplishment

RARELY INFLUENTIAL	OCCASIONALLY INFLUENTIAL	ALWAYS INFLUENTIAL

Environmental/Animal Protection

RARELY INFLUENTIAL	OCCASIONALLY INFLUENTIAL	ALWAYS INFLUENTIAL

Helping Others

RARELY INFLUENTIAL	OCCASIONALLY INFLUENTIAL	ALWAYS INFLUENTIAL

Creativity

RARELY INFLUENTIAL	OCCASIONALLY INFLUENTIAL	ALWAYS INFLUENTIAL

Wealth

RARELY INFLUENTIAL   OCCASIONALLY INFLUENTIAL   ALWAYS INFLUENTIAL

Physical Activity

RARELY INFLUENTIAL   OCCASIONALLY INFLUENTIAL   ALWAYS INFLUENTIAL

Justice and Ethics

RARELY INFLUENTIAL   OCCASIONALLY INFLUENTIAL   ALWAYS INFLUENTIAL

Pursuit of Knowledge

RARELY INFLUENTIAL   OCCASIONALLY INFLUENTIAL   ALWAYS INFLUENTIAL

Spirituality/Faith

RARELY INFLUENTIAL   OCCASIONALLY INFLUENTIAL   ALWAYS INFLUENTIAL

Health

RARELY INFLUENTIAL   OCCASIONALLY INFLUENTIAL   ALWAYS INFLUENTIAL

Balance with Family/Play Outside of Work

RARELY INFLUENTIAL   OCCASIONALLY INFLUENTIAL   ALWAYS INFLUENTIAL

Other value that I frequently consider: _____

RARELY INFLUENTIAL   OCCASIONALLY INFLUENTIAL   ALWAYS INFLUENTIAL

Other value that I frequently consider: _____

RARELY INFLUENTIAL   OCCASIONALLY INFLUENTIAL   ALWAYS INFLUENTIAL

From this exercise you should be able to see that your values will shape the decisions you make. Take a look at which values fall into each of the three influence sections. Were there any surprises? What conclusions can you draw from the results? Knowing your values can help you make life choices that are congruent with what is important to you. It can also highlight when values conflict, helping you understand associated feelings of distress and loss. In the next exercise, you'll get the chance to see how your values are currently taking shape in your work life.

Evaluating Your Current Circumstances

Considering the values from pages 86 and 87, you can now assess how your current circumstances fit with your values. What three values from the previous exercise are the most influential? Label them in the blanks below.

Now assess how your current work (paid or unpaid) or pursuit of work fits with your top values (1 = *Not Congruent with Current Work* to 10 = *Fully Congruent with Current Work*).

Value 1: _____

_____

0   5   10

Value 2: _____

_____

0   5   10

Value 3: _____

_____

0   5   10

Evaluate each value separately.

SCORE 5–10

Congratulations! You are in or working toward a role that allows you to function within your values system. While 10 is the ideal, few things in life can exist in ideal form. Anything above 5 means that, more often than not, you are engaging this value while making a living, and that is a wonderful thing.

SCORE 0–4

More often than not, your work is incongruent with this value.

How does this discrepancy affect you emotionally, mentally, and/or physically?

_____

_____

_____

_____

What factors contribute to this incongruence? (Example: family pressure, financial necessity, visa status, fear of failure)

_____

_____

_____

_____

If you cannot find a new job right now, are there ways to incorporate these values into your life currently? (Example: reframing your work in light of the above values, setting long-term goals, or finding activities outside of work to fulfill these.)

_____

_____

_____

_____

Values are a fluid and changing construct in life, and your top values may shift based on context and need. Taking time every so often to assess whether you are pursuing work that is meaningful for your life can either help affirm your choices or help you redirect your efforts.

COMMON CHALLENGES

HSPs tend to be highly influenced by values such as work/life balance and caring for others. This can lead to misunderstanding and conflict with non-HSPs when making work choices. It is not uncommon for an HSP to consider quality-of-life factors (e.g., vacation time, coworker personalities, ethics of the company) when deciding on employment. So when they decide to take work that pays less in order to prioritize mental, emotional, and/or physical well-being, the people around them may be critical.

It is common for someone to seek guidance from a mentor or therapist because they feel stuck in their decision-making process. Often when experiencing indecision, others' opinions may weigh heavily on the mind of the HSP—opinions such as "you will regret not taking this lucrative opportunity" or "you'd be a fool to pass this up." These messages cause anxiety for the HSP. There is a fine line between thought-provoking questions that help you evaluate all aspects of a decision and questions that feel critical and judgmental.

When making decisions around work, choose your advisers carefully. Consider what values shape the adviser's decisions (e.g., money) and whether this matches with your own values set (e.g., quality of life). Take in the concern expressed by others and ask if you have missed any considerations, and then evaluate their concern within your own values. Seek consultation from a variety of trusted advisers while giving space for your own intuition. Regardless of what choice you make, know *why* you are making that decision.

Remember, sharing your process with others is not the same as needing to justify yourself. If you find yourself feeling defensive or unsupported, take time to reflect on why (for example, are you feeling insecure in your choices or are they being unnecessarily critical?). Inviting others into your decision-making process makes you highly vulnerable; choose people who are respectful and not just those who will agree with you.

Environmental Considerations

Just like your environment at home can be curated to support relaxation, your environment at work can be curated to support your performance. On page 91, you will find environmental considerations laid out in an either/or fashion to help you identify preferences. You may prefer a balance of the options, which is useful information.

PACE OF WORK	Deadlines are relaxed	OR	Race against the clock
CONSISTENCY OF WORK	Steady flow	OR	Seasonal ebb and flow
INTELLECTUAL CHALLENGE	I know what I'm doing	OR	I love solving puzzles
CUSTOMER INTERACTION	Behind the scenes	OR	Client-facing
COMMUTE	Closer the better	OR	I'll drive if I love it
EARNINGS	Consistent paycheck	OR	Variability with chance for higher pay
SCHEDULE	Routine and structure	OR	Variety and adventure
MANAGEMENT	Clear expectations	OR	Autonomy and creativity
NOISE LEVEL	Shhhh, please	OR	Silence is distracting
RECOGNITION	No feedback means good feedback	OR	Feedback leads to growth
ANALYTICAL THINKING	Tell me what I need to know	OR	Give me the data and I'll draw conclusions
PHYSICAL ACTIVITY	Chill and low effort	OR	Up and moving
CREATIVITY	Routine/expected	OR	Art improves everything
INNOVATION	If it works, leave it be	OR	Change is necessary for growth
VARIETY	Few tasks/roles	OR	Multiple tasks/roles

Sometimes breaking things into either/or categories can help you identify preferences you weren't aware of. These answers may not *always* be true but can help improve self-understanding.

REFLECTING ON PAST EXPERIENCES

Depending on what circumstances you were born into, work may have been seen as a fun, voluntary pursuit; a nonoptional, harsh reality of life; or perhaps something more in the middle, where the quality of work and life were more balanced. This framing affects how you went through school and what work options you saw as viable for your life. If you grew up in poverty, then finding a job may be less about finding a sense of meaning and more about avoiding the hardships of financial insecurity. Alternatively, if you grew up in financial wealth, work may be focused on finding a sense of meaning.

Because HSPs absorb the environment and emotions around them, you likely picked up on a number of implicit messages that your caretaker(s) may not even have endorsed consciously. For example, Jay noticed every day that his mother came home after work to collapse on the couch for an hour before starting dinner. His mother would talk about how much she loved being a nurse and helping other people. Jay noticed, however, that his mother was often exhausted, and her feet would hurt so badly that she would skip out on family events on the weekend. Jay realized from a young age that he wanted a job that would allow him to feel good physically, so he would not miss out on family events. In this case, Jay intuitively started identifying ways that his values and his mother's values were different.

Depending on the messages you picked up on implicitly and explicitly, you may feel a sense of conflict around having different values from your caregiver(s) and family of origin. For many families, these conflicts are difficult but not uncommon. Therefore, knowing more about how the values differ and the impact that difference has is valuable for both you and your family.

Early Messages

Here you will reflect on the home where you grew up and how it shaped your views on work. Consider what type of language was used around work. Think about what was communicated to you directly and what you picked up on through observation. Explore the following questions:

» *How many people in your family worked?* _____

    Did you have a caretaker who could stay home with you? _____

    How was gender discussed around work and family expectations? _____

    _____

    _____

    _____

» *How was money perceived and talked about?* _____

_____

_____

_____

    Was it talked about as a scarce resource? _____

    Were those finances kept individual or seen as shared by the family unit?

    _____

» *What values shaped job searching?* _____

_____

_____

_____

How do your current values from the previous exercise fit with the values of your family of origin? _____

» *What intersectional factors contribute to work experiences in your family? (Consider: ethnicity, faith/religion, socioeconomic status, ability status, generation, immigration status, rural/urban job availability, gender identity, sexual orientation, education level)*

_____
_____
_____
_____
_____

How did these factors influence employment status?

_____

How did these factors influence experiences in the workplace (e.g., interpersonal interactions, opportunities for advancement)?

_____
_____
_____

Reflecting on areas that you may have learned vicariously through your parents or other family members can be helpful in identifying underlying beliefs. These messages and beliefs may be shaping your journey through work, and being aware of them can be helpful.

Appreciation Over Obligation

When reflecting on your family of origin and work habits, it can be easy to minimize your own needs and wants. When taking your family into consideration as you plan your future, it can be helpful to keep a framework of choice. If you prioritize money for your family over something you value more, it can be easy to grow resentful. You always have a choice. Some of the choices have drastic consequences, but they are still choices. Remembering that you have a choice helps you maintain a sense of agency and can help mitigate feeling resentful over time.

How much does your family of origin influence your career choices?

_____

_____

How distressing do you find their opinions and expectations?

_____

_____

In what ways do you hide your wants or needs to avoid conflict around career choices?

_____

_____

_____

What holds you back from sharing your goals or desires with family?

_____

_____

_____

What consequences might you face if you choose something your family dislikes?

_____

_____

_____

In your current circumstances, how do you choose to move forward? Which values do you choose to prioritize right now, knowing that this may change in time?

_____

_____

_____

Family can be a mixture of support and stress, including when you are making decisions about your future. Being mindful of what, when, and how to share with them can help you manage feelings of discomfort.

Highly Sensitive People in the Workplace

HSPs are often highly attuned to any deficits they might have, which can lead to minimizing and dismissing their strengths in the workplace. There are a number of skills HSPs typically bring to the table, and, like in relationships, it becomes a matter of finding the right fit for your work. Being aware of your strengths can help balance negative feedback and help you grow professionally. If you employ someone who is highly sensitive, keep in mind that recognition of accomplishments and strengths is a valuable tool. Being seen and valued is a strong motivator for HSPs and goes a long way to improving morale and employee engagement.

Workplace Superpowers

Take a moment to reflect on your work. Think about the times you feel competent, capable, and content with your work, no matter how small the example might feel. Keep in mind that you have skills, whether or not they are acknowledged by other people—do not be afraid to validate yourself. Place a check mark next to the skills you identify with and then add your own.

☐ Spotting and fixing mistakes

☐ Soft skills and people management

☐ Hard skills specific to the job

☐ High frustration tolerance (can keep working on a problem despite setbacks)

☐ Recognizing trends in the field

☐ Anticipating needs of clients or bosses

☐ Improve morale through encouraging others

☐ Team player, good collaborator

☐ Attention to fine detail

☐ Follow rules and ethical guidelines closely

☐ High productivity when in my ideal stimulation zone

☐ Other: _____

» What do you bring to your role that others might not?

_____

_____

_____

» What parts of your job do you excel at and enjoy the most?

_____

_____

_____

» Are there ways you can be utilized more effectively in your current role?

_____

_____

_____

You may not be able to give yourself a raise, but knowing your value is important, especially when others cannot or will not see it. Knowing your value and being able to validate yourself is important in the workplace, as it is in other areas. It is always nice to be appreciated, but depending on your workplace and colleagues, this may not happen. Don't be afraid to be proud of who you are.

COMMON CHALLENGES

Many HSPs enjoy and value the content of their work but struggle when it comes to the context of the job. Being observed, receiving negative feedback, conflict, and environmental stressors can all be challenges in the workplace.

INTERPERSONAL CHALLENGES. HSPs often perform worse when being observed, which can make open offices, presentations, or annual reviews particularly stressful. It can help to build in transition time before and after stressful interactions, communicate with your boss about how to manage feedback, or request a follow-up meeting after a review so that you can take the verbal and written feedback home, digest it, and come back with any questions or concerns.

Keep in mind that work feedback is not (or should not be) personal. It should be about whether you are performing your job duties sufficiently. With constructive feedback, you should be able to know how you are doing and what concrete behavioral markers your boss is assessing. Refocusing on the behavior can help you avoid being caught up in the emotions of the other person and focus on the factors that are within your control.

ENVIRONMENTAL STRESSORS. The environment around you can contribute to concentration difficulties, sensory overwhelm, and exhaustion. Many HSPs benefit from assessing their environment, what is within their control, and how they can respond. If the fluorescent lights overhead lead to headaches, can you bring in a lamp or get blue-light-blocking glasses? Are headphones or earplugs an option if noise distracts you? Included in this can be how your workflow is structured. Many HSPs find a constant influx of emails to be distracting and overstimulating. Structuring your workday to include correspondence windows can be helpful, as can filtering your email. Get creative with where you input adaptive measures.

The People You See Every Day

The people you interact with daily can have a significant impact on your quality of life. If you have ever worked with a really strong personality, you likely know how one person can lift or crush the culture of a workplace. Here are some questions to ask yourself about potential work environments.

Do colleagues see one another as competition or support?

_____

_____

How much diversity do you see in the workplace? Consider diversity of ideas, culture, beliefs, ethnicities, abilities, family types, etc.

_____

_____

_____

How is feedback given and received between boss and employee and among colleagues?

_____

_____

_____

What level of friendship seems present in colleagues?

_____

_____

What level of friendship are you comfortable with in the workplace? (Another way to ask this: How rigid do you prefer boundaries to be in the workplace?)

_____

_____

_____

What are the management styles of the people with whom you will be working?

_____

_____

_____

Does feedback occur publicly or privately?

_____

_____

_____

Are these people you might be able to trust? What does your intuition tell you?

_____

_____

_____

Assessing the interpersonal dynamics of a potential new job can be an important part of the interview process. Anytime you go for an interview, remember that you are also interviewing them and gathering information so that you can make an informed decision.

Transitions

Switching between your professional roles and personal roles requires space for decompressing, shifting to a different mind-set, and recovery from draining activities. Work can be both exhausting and rewarding. Take a moment to think about your transition routine around work.

How do you currently transition from work to personal life at the end of the workday?

_____

_____

_____

_____

Are there fuzzy boundaries between work and personal life that make it difficult to disconnect (e.g., being expected to respond to emails when at home)?

_____

_____

_____

_____

What are the aspects of your work that result in high stress? How do you currently process them?

_____

_____

_____

_____

Can you think of one or two ways you can be more intentional about transitioning between roles (e.g., taking a five-minute meditation break in the car before driving home)?

_____

_____

_____

_____

If you lack space and time to recover from or manage the draining portions of your work, then burnout may ensue, leaving you tempted to walk away from that work altogether. Noticing the draining portions and intervening early can allow for sustained engagement in your current work.

REFLECTING ON PAST EXPERIENCES

It is common for the past to show up in two key ways for HSPs in the workplace. First, when dynamics from your early life (think parents or siblings) play out with coworkers or bosses. For example, if your parents were highly critical and contributed to high anxiety, then receiving negative feedback from your boss may feel very similar regardless of your boss's intent. As a result, your emotional reaction to and internalization of the feedback may feel much more intense than you expected going into the meeting. Similarly, feelings of competition or rivalry that you had with siblings may reappear with coworkers. These feelings can make it difficult to discern between what is "your stuff" (heightened feelings of criticism) and "their stuff" (your boss lacking warmth). Therapy can be a great tool for sorting through these tangled emotions.

Second, managing past workplace trauma is another common HSP workplace theme. Sometimes this is _Trauma_ (i.e., objective traumas like assault) and sometimes it is _trauma_ (i.e., subjective traumas like verbal teasing). Trauma of any kind activates the sympathetic nervous system into fight-flight-freeze. Once someone is removed from the source of trauma, the work of healthy processing involves re-creating a sense of safety and trust. When people encounter a stimulus that reminds them of past trauma, they can easily be triggered back into fight-flight-freeze. Because you cannot choose when you or others are triggered into fight-flight-freeze, remember to practice compassion and to get help if it impairs your ability to function effectively.

CHAPTER RECAP

Work makes up a large portion of life for most people and can be an area where you experience less agency in your choices. As you move through your life, your relationship with work will be ever-changing. It can be helpful at various stages to refresh yourself on the following:

1. Living congruent with your values is key to feeling fulfilled. Assessing how your current work measures up and mapping pathways toward increased congruence can help you achieve a sense of fulfillment in life.

2. Knowing your skills and your value is helpful internally for validation and self-esteem. It is also helpful externally for negotiating, self-advocacy, and advancing in your career.

3. Trauma can affect you in the workplace. Seek help if you find past experiences interfering with the life you want.

CHAPTER FIVE

Health and Self-Care

Your body is sensitive and will respond accordingly to hunger, tiredness, or overwhelm. When feeling poorly, it will speak up loudly and ask you to take care of it. While this can be inconvenient, it also means that your body is constantly giving you useful feedback. Think of your body as having good communication skills to help keep you in your optimal functioning zone. This chapter will touch on the ways stress affects the body, the value of mindfulness, and effective coping strategies for preventive healthcare.

Highly Sensitive People and Healthcare

Responding to your body when it becomes overstimulated is important for your long-term health. When you are overstimulated, your brain assesses the presence of threats to your well-being and can activate your sympathetic nervous system (fight-flight-freeze) in order to keep you safe. In the short term, this is an incredibly effective way to ensure survival. When this becomes a constant state, it can lead to chronic anxiety. Because HSPs are more prone to being negatively affected by stress and negative environments, it is common to experience anxiety disorders and illnesses (Goldberg et al., 2018).

When dealing with chronic anxiety and stress, your body is constantly producing stress hormones (e.g., acetylcholine and adrenaline), which can contribute to chronic inflammation in the body and worsen health conditions, such as autoimmune disorders (Pongratz and Straub, 2014). The more often your sympathetic nervous system is triggered, and the longer it is activated, the harder it becomes to calm it down. If you have a history of traumatic experiences or chronic stress due to family, work, or school, it may take longer for you to begin training your parasympathetic nervous system, which pulls you out of fight-flight-freeze. But it is possible!

This reciprocal nature of psychological and physical well-being has been the foundation behind the rise of mindfulness exercises in clinical and social settings (Greeson et al., 2018). Mindfulness practices, like meditation or yoga, activate your parasympathetic nervous system. This is why every doctor, therapist, or healer you have seen recently has likely recommended that you begin meditating. This is not a replacement for medical intervention, but it will maximize your efforts toward health.

Because your body is more likely to be affected by stressors, it also means that interventions can be particularly effective. This means that you may be more affected by certain medications. Many HSPs report either higher side effect rates or needing lower doses of medication. Additionally, maintaining healthy patterns around sleep, nutrition, and exercise are essential tools for your health. For example, Yano and Oishi found that exercise helped moderate the relationship between depression and being an HSP (2018). Skipping sleep, eating inflammatory foods, and not exercising are all surefire ways to undermine your health.

Please note that some physical conditions can present similarly to HSP, such as Ehlers-Danlos syndrome (EDS), a collection of genetic variants that affect connective tissue. Many people with EDS grow up hearing similar messages (e.g., "you are too sensitive") and experiencing similar sensory overwhelm, especially around sensations inside their bodies. In fact, most people with EDS report being highly sensitive, though no formal research exists to date. It can be important not to write off any health concerns as "I'm just being sensitive" and make sure you get proper medical care for any symptoms you are experiencing.

Body Awareness

Learning to listen to your body is a skill that needs to be fostered or reconnected to after years of silencing what your body has been trying to tell you. In this exercise you will begin reconnecting with your body. Allow yourself 15 to 20 minutes for this exercise.

1. Find a comfortable space to sit or lie. You may want to put on some calm background music, as long as it does not distract you.

2. Breathe deeply. Slowly increase the depth of your breathing, increasing from shallow, in-your-chest breaths to deep belly or diaphragm breaths. Feel the air filling your lungs and the muscles release when you breathe out and your abdomen deflates. Do this 10 times. As you continue the exercise, keep your breathing deep and rhythmic.

3. Shift your attention toward your body. The goal is not to judge or fix, merely to listen and notice where your body stores stress and tension.

4. Start with your head (eyebrows, jaws, scalp) and notice any places of tightness or discomfort where you may be holding stress. As you breathe in, gather that tension, and as you breathe out, allow your muscles to release.

5. As you continue breathing deeply, work your way through your body, taking two to three deep breaths focused on each area, releasing tension each time you breathe out.

6. Scan the following areas:

Neck	Hands	Hips
Shoulders	Upper back	Thighs
Upper arms	Lower back	Calves
Lower arms	Abdomen	Feet

7. When you have scanned the last section, notice how your whole body feels. You might feel tired or relaxed. Bring yourself back to the present by noticing the environment around you. Wiggle your fingers and toes and slowly wake your body back up.

Taking brief, intentional breaks to check in with your body helps with regulating anxiety, calming the sympathetic nervous system, and noticing potential problem areas early. As you become more familiar with where and how you hold stress, you can begin being mindful of those areas proactively.

Mindfulness Takeaways

Take a moment to reflect on what your body communicated to you in the previous exercise.

What was tight, tired, or sore?

_____

_____

_____

Did anything feel restless or unsettled?

_____

_____

_____

_____

What areas, if any, need attention?

_____

_____

_____

_____

Are there things you can do today or tomorrow to help with any discomfort (e.g., exercise, a hot bath)?

_____

_____

_____

_____

Are there any long-standing pains or discomfort that need follow-up with a professional (e.g., doctor, physical therapist, massage therapist)? What has been holding you back from acting on this?

_____

_____

_____

_____

_____

_____

_____

Incorporating a body-scan mindfulness practice daily or weekly can be an excellent way of checking in with your body and responding to needs before they become problematic.

COMMON CHALLENGES

Being dismissed by doctors is one of the most common challenges HSPs face in navigating healthcare. Doctors may dismiss the severity or existence of symptoms and medication side effects. Many HSPs who take psychiatric medication benefit from subclinical (very low) doses of the medication or need much slower tapering on or off of the medication. It can be particularly difficult to advocate for your needs when a doctor tells you that your concerns are invalid or that your symptoms are "statistically unlikely."

This dismissive response from doctors can teach you to distrust your body and can leave you feeling dread, hurt, or overwhelm that then becomes paired with medical experiences. These negative experiences may lead you to avoid seeking help. HSPs are often able to perceive things in their bodies that the average person would not. Learning to trust your experience is crucial to your receiving proper medical treatment. If you have lost touch with this awareness of your body, learning to reconnect with it will be an important part of your journey toward health. Remember, too, that there are limits to how doctors and medicine can help you. For example, if you find that you feel poorly after eating gluten but you test negative for gluten allergy, it does not mean that gluten does not affect you. What is measurable in the scientific community does not always correlate with individual experience, so listening to your body and responding to your needs accordingly is something only you can fully do. Ideally this includes input from trusted professionals.

REFLECTING ON PAST EXPERIENCES

Depending on your medical journey, the intersection with your HSP trait may vary greatly. If you have a co-occurring chronic health journey, there may be a high level of subjective and objective trauma related to past medical experiences. Whether you are generally healthy or have chronic health challenges, a common theme for HSPs is discomfort when speaking up about their health, which often relates back to childhood experiences.

Many HSP children can pick up on their needs being inconvenient for other people. For example, if your caretaker had to stay home from work when you were sick, or if money was tight and going to the doctor was an unexpected expense, you may have internalized the message that your needs are inconvenient, even harmful to your family. HSP children may pick up on the distress in their caretaker's body language or tone of voice and internalize that their needs are disruptive to others. As a result, you may have learned how to keep quiet, manage yourself, and avoid disrupting the flow of life in your household. As an adult, it can be easy to continue this pattern and prioritize the comfort of others over your own needs, to the detriment of your health. The goal is, at minimum, to see your needs or wants as equally valid to the needs or wants of others.

Reflecting on Your Health Journey

Health can be a fraught topic for HSPs. Reflecting on your journey can help you process painful experiences and move you toward acceptance and self-advocacy.

Think back through your health journey. There are two facets of your journey to assess: the physical experiences and the messages you took in. Take a few minutes to sit in a quiet, reflective space and let your mind wander around the theme of your health journey.

Pick one memory that sticks out to you and write about it briefly here.

_____

_____

_____

_____

_____

What emotions come along with this memory?

_____

_____

_____

_____

Do you recall times when you minimized your health needs?

_____

_____

_____

_____

Or times when you downplayed symptoms?

_____

_____

_____

_____

What was your motivation behind downplaying or minimizing?

_____

_____

_____

_____

What would have been helpful for you to hear or experience in that moment?

_____

_____

_____

What was helpful during these times (e.g., emotionally and physically)?

_____

_____

_____

How did your family talk about health?

_____

_____

_____

_____

What are ways that your intersecting identities may have influenced these experiences (e.g., racial minorities, people with disabilities, religious beliefs)?

_____

_____

_____

_____

When you are sick now, what do you need?

_____

_____

_____

_____

It can be common to feel embarrassed or guilty when your body responds out of sensitivity, like getting hives easily. Assessing your past experiences can help bring insight into how you handle your health today. Whether other people understand or validate your experience, remember that you know your body best, you live within that body, and you have the right to care for it and yourself the best way you know how.

Highly Sensitive People and Self-Care

Somewhere between childhood and adulthood, there can be a shift into thinking that you should be able to do everything. In reality, all people have limitations. The HSP experience deviates from the non-HSP experience in that the consequences to ignoring limitations may be experienced more intensely, especially around physical limitations. A helpful practice is feeling some separation between your sense of identity and your body. Beginning to see your body as its own entity, like a dependent child, can help introduce self-compassion. You would not get angry at a child for feeling hungry or tired; you would respond to those needs as best you could. Consider responding to your body similarly. Each time a need pops up, there is an opportunity for teachable moments where you can learn how to care for your body more effectively.

As you listen to your body and respond, you can develop strategies for self-care. This can be a challenging term depending on your cultural background. *Self-care* refers to intentional practices that help manage stress, promote health, and find balance between different parts of your identity. Taking time to exercise, be in nature, eat nutritious food, and get proper sleep are forms of self-care that everyone can benefit from.

Other forms of self-care may be more subjective. If you have a straightforward, concrete job but are creative at heart, making time for art projects or classes may be important for you. If socializing is particularly stressful, setting limits on social outings for the week might be a form of self-care. Alternatively, if time with friends helps manage stress levels, scheduling a weekly get-together might be a priority. Self-care can vary in expense, time, or energy requirements and be tailored according to various levels of resources.

Finding Your Movement

There are innumerable options for exercise programs in today's culture, many focused on high cardio and maximum calorie burning. This can be great for some, but not all HSPs enjoy intense workouts, class settings, or fast-paced environments. Evaluate what you need in an exercise routine and environment and find ways to access this.

What benefits do I notice from exercising?

_____

_____

_____

_____

What goals do I have for exercise (e.g., increased strength, overall wellness, running a marathon, losing or gaining weight)?

_____

_____

_____

_____

Given my exercise goals, how much exercise works for me? If you are just starting out, build in gradual increases and consider working with a professional.

Frequency: _____

Duration: _____

What types of exercises help me feel grounded, energetic, and healthy?

_____

_____

_____

What are current barriers to implementing an exercise routine?

_____

_____

_____

What happens when I stop exercising or skip sessions?

_____

_____

_____

How can I prioritize this as part of my medical care rather than see it as an optional hobby?

_____

_____

_____

Exercise has medicinal effects. There is a wide variety of what type of exercise works for different people, but all doctors and researchers agree: Moving your body is important. And if you're not typically in the habit of getting exercise, it might take a couple of different trial runs to find the right fit—the type of movement that leaves you feeling grounded and energized, contented and invigorated.

Nurturing Nutrition

What you put in your body matters. This is the source of fuel for your body, and the quality of nutrients taken in will affect how well the system functions. One challenge is that what works for one person's body may not work for another.

Many HSPs have food sensitivities. Tracking your food and monitoring how food affects you can be a helpful practice for many HSPs. Telling you what to eat is beyond the scope of this book; however, use the following as a template to track how food makes you *feel* physically and emotionally.

Glasses of water are listed to help you track whether you are hydrated and how this may contribute to how you feel.

SUNDAY

TIME OF DAY	HOW I FEEL BEFORE I EAT	FOODS EATEN	GLASSES OF WATER	HOW I FEEL IMMEDIATELY AFTER I EAT	HOW I FEEL 3–4 HOURS AFTER MY MEAL

MONDAY

TIME OF DAY	HOW I FEEL BEFORE I EAT	FOODS EATEN	GLASSES OF WATER	HOW I FEEL IMMEDIATELY AFTER I EAT	HOW I FEEL 3–4 HOURS AFTER MY MEAL

TUESDAY

TIME OF DAY	HOW I FEEL BEFORE I EAT	FOODS EATEN	GLASSES OF WATER	HOW I FEEL IMMEDIATELY AFTER I EAT	HOW I FEEL 3–4 HOURS AFTER MY MEAL

WEDNESDAY

TIME OF DAY	HOW I FEEL BEFORE I EAT	FOODS EATEN	GLASSES OF WATER	HOW I FEEL IMMEDIATELY AFTER I EAT	HOW I FEEL 3-4 HOURS AFTER MY MEAL

THURSDAY

TIME OF DAY	HOW I FEEL BEFORE I EAT	FOODS EATEN	GLASSES OF WATER	HOW I FEEL IMMEDIATELY AFTER I EAT	HOW I FEEL 3–4 HOURS AFTER MY MEAL

FRIDAY

TIME OF DAY	HOW I FEEL BEFORE I EAT	FOODS EATEN	GLASSES OF WATER	HOW I FEEL IMMEDIATELY AFTER I EAT	HOW I FEEL 3–4 HOURS AFTER MY MEAL

SATURDAY

TIME OF DAY	HOW I FEEL BEFORE I EAT	FOODS EATEN	GLASSES OF WATER	HOW I FEEL IMMEDIATELY AFTER I EAT	HOW I FEEL 3–4 HOURS AFTER MY MEAL

Track this information for one week and explore the following questions:

» Are there correlations between certain foods and certain emotions? (e.g., Do I get anxiety two to three hours after I eat sugar or caffeine? Do I tend to overeat when I feel sad?)

_____

_____

_____

_____

_____

_____

_____

» Are there physical symptoms that correspond to foods?

Common food groups to pay attention to for possible sensitivities: dairy, gluten, lectins, nightshades (tomatoes, eggplants, etc.), processed sugars, sugar substitutes, alcohol, processed meats, cooking oils.

Physical symptoms to watch for: feeling nervous, heart palpitations, heart rate increases, tremors, stomach pain or discomfort, heartburn, sweating, increased hunger, irritability, headaches, fatigue, mental confusion, disrupted focus, tiredness.

_____

_____

_____

_____

_____

_____

_____

» What meals or foods helped me feel my best?

_____

_____

_____

_____

_____

» How can I incorporate more of these foods?

_____

_____

_____

_____

_____

_____

» Am I getting enough protein, healthy fats, fiber, vitamins, and complex carbohydrates? (This is highly variable based on health needs, exercise, body makeup, etc. Consider working with a professional to discern what your needs are.)

_____

_____

_____

_____

_____

Food is your fuel, and selecting fuel that optimizes your functioning helps set you up for success every day. Balancing guidelines, enjoyment, and health can be a fluid process; just remember to check in with your body and make intentional choices.

COMMON CHALLENGES

When HSPs grow up with the idea that their sensitivities are bad, engaging in self-care practices that help with those sensitivities can easily become paired with shame. This may be reinforced if people around you are judgmental of or not understanding of your self-care needs.

For example, if you need nine hours of sleep, your colleague might say, "Oh, that must be nice, but I have too much work to do." The message here is that if you valued work as much as this colleague, you would not be sleeping so much. An HSP might be considered "weak," "lazy," or "selfish" because they prioritize sleep. How people respond to your self-care methods likely says more about them than it does about you. This colleague may feel resentful that you have a practice that is nurturing and that they have not figured out how to do the same. Their judgment is not a battle you need to take on, and neither is their self-care. You can manage only your own behavior and choices.

Another common misconception is that self-care is something for rich, privileged people. While money can broaden access to certain self-care options, it is not an essential ingredient to self-care. There are many intentional practices you can incorporate that are inexpensive or free. Living within your means and avoiding comparison to others are also forms of self-care, as they can allow you to be present and grateful for what you have.

Self-Care for a More Effective You

Self-care is not an indulgent, selfish act. Rather, it is an empowering, necessary part of life that allows you to be the best version of yourself. By extension, it means you can better care for others as well. As you continue getting to know yourself, consider planning "dates" with yourself where you can continue deepening your knowledge of and appreciation for yourself. Following are some examples of dates and self-care exercises that are free or inexpensive. Pick one to try out this week.

☐ Go for coffee somewhere new

☐ Go for a hike or nature walk

☐ Plan a night in to binge-watch a good show

☐ Take a short nap

- [ ] Draw a hot bath, light a candle, and play relaxing music
- [ ] Do a guided meditation
- [ ] Journal
- [ ] Go to the mall or park and people watch
- [ ] Draw or color
- [ ] Meal prep for the week
- [ ] Organize or clean out a space you use regularly
- [ ] Do a gentle stretching routine
- [ ] Write a gratitude list
- [ ] Try a new makeup, hair, or fashion look
- [ ] Dance
- [ ] Watch your favorite childhood movie
- [ ] Eat breakfast
- [ ] Listen to a podcast
- [ ] Watch online tutorials to practice a new skill
- [ ] Turn your phone off or to Do Not Disturb mode for an evening
- [ ] Bake something yummy
- [ ] Cuddle with a pet or comfy blanket
- [ ] Call a friend
- [ ] Write a thank-you card or note to someone
- [ ] Go to your local library and check out a book
- [ ] Many museums have free days—research this and schedule a date to visit
- [ ] Get up early one morning with your favorite hot beverage

What are some of your favorite self-care practices? After practicing one or two of these for a few weeks, what changes have you noticed, if any, in your sense of well-being?

_____

_____

_____

_____

Getting to know yourself, like getting to know anyone, takes time and space. It is okay, even good, to get to know yourself and care for yourself. Ultimately, this will make you a better friend, partner, sibling, worker, etc.—it benefits everyone.

PRIORITIZING SLEEP

Sleep is essential for maintaining good health. Aiming for 7–9 hours of sleep each night is the goal for most adults, but every person is different and some HSPs may need closer to 10 (especially when accounting for transition times around sleep). You will also need extra sleep any time you are recovering from high stress or illness. Good sleep hygiene practices include:

- Consistent sleep and wake times (including on the weekend)
- Turning off screens 1–2 hours before bed
- Having a bedtime routine that signals to your body that you are winding down for the day
- Exposure to natural light during the day to help with circadian rhythm (blue light therapy can be helpful for those without access to natural daylight)
- Limiting substances like alcohol, sugar, or caffeine if they interfere with your sleep

If you are practicing good sleep hygiene and continue to feel exhausted or have trouble getting out of bed each morning, please seek medical advice as this can be a sign of underlying health concerns.

A common association HSPs and non-HSPs have with self-care is that it is selfish. This comes from intersecting cultural messages and leads to guilt and shame around self-care. Due to their sensitivity to implicit and explicit messages, HSPs are more likely to internalize guilt and shame on a deep level. Keep in mind that there will be generational and cultural differences between you and whoever raised you. This awareness can help you hold a space of compassion for yourself and others as you reflect on how self-care was discussed, modeled, or evaluated where you grew up.

An example of an explicit negative message can come from religious backgrounds wherein you are instructed to always consider others before yourself. Practically, however, this will inevitably lead to burnout and diminish your ability to care for others. An example of an implicit message is observing how your caretakers engaged in self-care. If you had a parent who worked two jobs and sacrificed their own food, health, sleep, and well-being, it can send confusing messages around self-care. If you are currently a caretaker, consider modeling self-care by inviting your children to go on a walk with you, set up a movie night together, or head into nature.

Self-Care vs. Selfishness

Guilt and shame can quickly sneak in and undermine efforts to take care of yourself. Being mindful of what constitutes selfishness and what helps you be a better friend, partner, colleague, or family member can help challenge negative beliefs around self-care.

What is a form of self-care that often leaves you feeling guilty?

_____

_____

Guilt is functional when one is doing something offensive, against the rules, or harmful to someone else. In what ways could this act of self-care be seen as harmful to someone else?

_____

_____

_____

Keep in mind that a lack of benefit to someone is not the same as being harmful. For example, your partner might say, "If you sleep for nine hours, I feel lonely after you go to bed." It is nice for your partner to have company, but their social wants are different from your physical needs.

Conversely, what are the benefits of this self-care? (Example: When I am well rested, I am more positive and engaged when I spend time with my partner, I perform better at work, I feel more confident, and I get sick less often.)

_____

_____

_____

As you look at the pros and cons of your act of self-care, do the pros outweigh the cons?

_____

_____

If no, is there another form of self-care that might be more effective?

_____

_____

If yes, would you expect a friend to feel guilt for a practice that provides these pros? Then can you extend the same grace to yourself?

_____

_____

Responding to yourself the same way you would to a friend can be a helpful reframe around matters of self-care. This is one way to incorporate self-compassion into your daily life, allowing you to take care of yourself in healthy ways.

CHAPTER RECAP

Health can be fickle for HSPs, but keeping the perspective of prevention rather than reaction is an empowering way to engage your health. Sleep, nutrition, and exercise are the building blocks of foundational health, and HSPs benefit from making these a priority. As you find your baseline health needs, remember the following:

1. Prioritizing sleep is paramount to short- and long-term health.

2. What you put into your body matters.

3. Exercise is good for your physical and mental well-being.

4. Nature benefits you in a multitude of ways.

5. Self-care is not selfish but ultimately benefits everyone with whom you come in contact.

CHAPTER SIX

Deeper Work

Going deeper in your work can be intimidating and hard but well worth it. For many HSPs, there are past wounds that continue to be reprocessed at different levels. The longer you live, the more experiences you have to process, and it can quickly become untenable. It can be appealing to hold out hope for repair in some relationships and that key figures in your life will come around to provide healing. One of the hardest lessons to learn can be that you must become your own best parent, advocate, and friend. You will explore ways to integrate painful memories and grow from them within the framework of gratefulness and self-compassion.

Healing Old Wounds

If you know people who have been through therapy, they will often say, "Therapy is hard work!" Revisiting past wounds, broken relationships, imperfections, and all the dark parts of life can be exhausting. At the same time, this practice can be integral to finding healthy functioning and being able to maximally enjoy life.

A helpful analogy is that of a broken bone. If someone quickly attends to the injury, they can reset the bone and it can heal (which always takes time). Once healed, it can return closely to previous functioning, or sometimes may even grow back stronger. But what happens when you break a bone and it cannot be treated? Your body will repair the bone as best it can, you will develop compensatory methods to maintain some level of functioning, and it will be recurrently painful. You will protect that injury from others for fear of the pain and potential worsening of the condition. When someone finally treats it, they may need to rebreak it in order to set it and help it heal in a more functional way. This is incredibly painful. Then you must endure physical therapy and relearn how to function. Once it has healed, you can begin moving toward growth and thriving—an exciting and time-consuming process. That can be how it feels to reopen past emotional wounds: painful, slow, and hard. This is one reason having a trained mental health provider walking through it with you is important.

In her book *Wisdom from the Couch*, psychoanalyst Dr. Jennifer Kunst (2014) lays out some of the most common themes that come up in therapy. She highlights topics such as unfairness, growth, acceptance, mortality, humility, and more with the beautiful and heartbreaking sides of each. For HSPs, these themes are the same but can resonate more deeply and take longer to process than for non-HSPs. Working through these themes involves a great deal of grief work and letting go of what could have been, past and present injustice, and the belief you can change people. Enduring that work opens the door to deep beauty, connection, hope, and meaning in life.

As you let go of the things that you cannot change and of self-criticism that does not move you toward improvement or health, it opens up space for new thoughts and experiences to fill you up. When your mind is filled with digesting past events, it can prevent new experiences from settling in; it is important to find a balance between processing the old and experiencing the new. You likely have many cringeworthy memories that make you critical of yourself. These critical responses are helpful only insofar as they move you toward growth and learning. When they stop serving that function, it is time to pivot toward coping. Practices such as self-compassion, challenging and reframing negative thoughts, and gratitude exercises can be helpful, as can working with a therapist.

Rewriting Your Narrative with Self-Compassion

The stories you tell yourself shape the experiences you have. If you see yourself as a burden, then anytime someone says "no" to you, you will interpret it through the lens of "I'm a burden." In short, language matters. In shifting your language, you can begin to shift your interpretation of key events.

Think back to a recent cringeworthy experience: the people, context, dialogue, and aftermath. Give yourself about five minutes to sit with the memory. If it feels intolerable, feel free to grab a favorite fidget object or go on a short walk while you process the memory, but stay in the memory.

_____

_____

_____

_____

_____

_____

_____

_____

_____

_____

_____

_____

_____

_____

_____

_____

_____

_____

_____

Think about your favorite genre of fiction and storytelling. You might even have a favorite fictional series. Now, rewrite your story with a different protagonist and in the genre of your choosing. Consider how this event fits into a larger character growth narrative for the protagonist.

_____

_____

_____

_____

_____

_____

_____

_____

_____

_____

_____

_____

_____

_____

_____

_____

_____

Chances are you used softer, more compassionate or intentional language for the fictional character. Invite yourself to begin using similar language toward understanding your own character growth and narrative arc.

COMPLEMENTARY APPROACHES

Physicians Dr. Bessel van der Kolk (2014) and Dr. Gabor Maté (2003) both provide useful insight and data around how stress and trauma present physically. A full review of the scientific theories around why this happens is outside the scope of this book, but the short version is that your emotional state and your physical state are linked. While this is true for the average population, consider HSPs at a heightened vulnerability to this. As such, consider that therapeutic interventions for your well-being include, but are not limited to, talk therapy. As a psychologist, I will always recommend therapy. It can be helpful to attend to both your physical needs and your emotions. Many HSPs benefit from some form of bodywork in conjunction with mental health work, although access to both types of resources is a privilege.

You have likely noticed that when you are stressed, you might hold tension in different parts of your body. People commonly hold stress in their shoulders and neck, for example. Frequent, excessive constriction of muscles, being frequently or consistently flooded with stress hormones (e.g., cortisol, adrenaline), or increased blood pressure are all examples of ways stress might play out in the body. So attending to your body contributes to holistic healing. It is not uncommon for people to have painful memories pop up when getting a massage or to begin crying as the body releases tension.

Musculoskeletal work (e.g., massage therapy, acupuncture, chiropractic work) can include a variety of interventions depending on your health, preferences, and what is available to you. The empirical validation for musculoskeletal interventions varies widely, so do your research and talk with your doctor to find what interventions you may want to try. As you begin your healing journey, physically and emotionally, there can be a process of breaking down (think of resetting the bone from the earlier analogy) before you begin building back up. When you feel ready to begin rebuilding, introducing physical therapy, a trainer, or an exercise community can be a way of moving from healing into thriving in your physical body.

Barriers to Healing

People tend to be more accepting of and compassionate toward physical healing than emotional healing. Using the language of physical wounds can help reframe the emotional healing process and the history of injuries you may hold.

If you have experienced multiple emotional "broken bones," it can be hard to know what to attend to first. Self-protection, fear, and overwhelm are examples of reasons you might have put off starting your healing journey. Understanding barriers to healing can help you take intentional next steps in your process. Everyone's journey will look different, and everyone will benefit from different interventions at various times.

Take a moment to reflect on the whole of your life and the wounds that need healing. Make a list of interventions that might be helpful.

Example: Reading a book on boundaries and codependency

_____

_____

Example: Start therapy

_____

_____

Looking at this list, what are barriers you face to starting on one or all of these?

Example: I usually watch TV instead of reading

_____

_____

Example: My work schedule makes it hard to find a consistent time for therapy

_____

_____

Example: My finances are tight

_____

_____

Keeping in mind that it's not realistic to do all of these at once, is there one barrier that you can start problem-solving for? Can you get a library card and look for free books? Can you search for therapists with telehealth services? Is there a community clinic that offers reduced-fee services? Consider choosing one barrier to work on over the next month, and when you complete one helpful intervention, consider returning to this list to start working on another.

COMMON CHALLENGES

HSPs wounded in childhood often lack self-trust. HSPs may hear recurrent messages that their sensitivity is a burden and that they are the problem in relationships. This can contribute to an inaccurate belief that the an HSP's perception of reality is wrong and that they need others to validate them before the HSP can trust what they feel.

HSP children seek reassurance, understanding, and containment from their caregiver but do not always receive it. As a child, you experience many strange sensations (think of hunger in an infant) and emotions (like frustration when you don't get what you want). A child looks to their caretaker to make sense of these experiences (containment). HSPs crave and need this processing help from their caregivers and without it can experience their emotions as overwhelming and chaotic. If an HSP does not learn how to process and contain their own emotions, they begin to seek this processing from other relationships. This can leave HSPs vulnerable to codependency or manipulation.

Another challenge for HSPs is blurry boundaries, which can lead to the HSP overabsorbing the emotions of others. Mirror neurons fire when people observe behavior or emotion in others. With heightened sensory processing in the central nervous system, your mirror neurons are heightened as well (Acevedo et al., 2014). Which means when you see someone stub a toe, you may feel a twinge of pain in your own toe. As a result, being around others' emotions can trigger those emotions for you. This is part of what makes you a good friend with heightened empathy, but it can also make it difficult to sort out whose emotion is whose. It can be helpful when you are experiencing strong emotions to double-check and see where those emotions are coming from.

Self-Parenting

Many of the exercises in this book invite you to engage with yourself in a more loving manner—essentially, engaging yourself as a loving parent would, a parent motivated to support you and who loves you enough to help you grow. In this vein, you will practice processing and containing emotions.

Take a few minutes to think back to a time of intense emotion you experienced as a child. (It is best to work through traumatic experiences with a professional, but many HSPs have memories of intense, nontraumatic emotional experiences.) Visualize your adult self kneeling down and compassionately speaking with your child self. Ask your child self the following, and write your responses from your child self:

»   Adult Self: What was going on before you became upset?

Child Self Response: _____

_____

_____

_____

»   Adult Self: What emotions were you feeling? List as many as you can.

Child Self Response: _____

_____

_____

_____

»   Adult Self: Is there an emotion behind the emotion?

Example: There is typically a feeling of hurt or shame underneath anger.

Child Self Response: _____

_____

_____

_____

» How can your adult self help your child self understand what happened? Write an empathic, validating reflection of the emotions you recorded as well as a compassionate understanding of what your child self is experiencing.

Example: I hear that you feel angry, embarrassed, and hurt that your friends laughed at you. Sometimes when we feel hurt, we lash out at the other person because we don't know how to express ourselves.

Adult Self Response: _____

_____

_____

_____

It is difficult to learn how to self-validate and contain your own emotions. This is a part of maturing emotionally and can be a great use of therapy if you find this type of activity particularly challenging.

Independent Assertiveness

Part of learning and implementing boundaries in relationships involves assertiveness. This can be an intimidating word for HSPs, introverts, and people pleasers. Thankfully, you can begin practicing this skill within yourself before bringing it into the relational context.

Reflect on the past few days and identify one thing you needed during this time (e.g., food, downtime, exercise). List it here:

_____

Imagine you are in conversation with someone and identify five ways you could state this need. Experiment with different levels of assertiveness, directness, and urgency.

1. _____

_____

_____

2. _____

_____

_____

3. _____

_____

_____

4. _____

_____

_____

5. _____

_____

_____

Circle the statement that feels most comfortable to you. Over the next week, anytime you notice that you need something, begin identifying it and explicitly labeling it to yourself in a similar manner.

Learning how to identify and label your needs is a large part of assertiveness, and you can practice this with yourself anytime. For example, the next time you feel hungry, say to yourself, "I feel hungry. I need to eat something." As you grow in this practice, begin removing phrasing that minimizes your needs, such as "I think I need," "maybe it would be good to," or any forms of apologizing for your needs.

Embracing the Learning Process

Many HSPs hold themselves (and others) to high standards. This can lead to feelings of shame and embarrassment when you make mistakes, especially when others witness them. You cannot be perfect, and you cannot know what you don't know. Thinking back to some of your "mistakes," practice reframing them in terms of what you learned. Add a statement of appreciation for this lesson.

MISTAKE: *I fumbled my presentation in front of the whole team.*

LESSON: *I would benefit from less coffee on presentation mornings and from reviewing my presentation a few more times before I present. I'm glad I know this now and look forward to trying something new next time.*

Mistake: _____

_____

Lesson: _____

_____

_____

_____

Mistake: _____

_____

_____

Lesson: _____

_____

_____

_____

Mistake: _____

_____

Lesson: _____

_____

_____

_____

Giving yourself permission to be imperfect and to be a lifelong learner can grant you space for growth and self-compassion.

> *Shame is a common response to mistakes and can be a useful emotion when it moves you to better behavior (e.g., I'm ashamed of how I yelled at Stacey; next time I want to respond differently). Shame ceases to be functional when it is associated with your value as a person (e.g., I yelled at Stacey; I'm ashamed of who I am; I don't deserve good friends).*

Managing and Thriving

Listening to stories from communities that you are not regularly exposed to can be a great way of building empathy and learning new ways to think about the world. One helpful takeaway from chronic illness communities is that it is okay to grieve what you have lost and to grant yourself permission to be different from others. To be clear, being an HSP is not an illness, but it does mean that you have unique needs around sensory input and processing. Humans are social creatures that desire to fit in. From an evolutionary perspective, fitting in allows one to survive. But consider, too, that the people society holds in high regard are those who walk their own path and are unafraid to be different. There will be times when fitting in serves an important function professionally and socially, yet there will be times when you must embrace your differences.

As you do the work of healing, you can move from surviving with this HSP trait into thriving. Surviving is a state wherein you are getting by from day to day, often feeling overwhelmed, depleted, or frazzled. Thriving is a state where you have effective coping strategies, are growing and improving, and are functioning in an optimized state most of the time. When you are thriving, you will have a healthy relationship with yourself marked by appreciation, warmth, and motivation to grow. You have already started the process of moving toward thriving by going through this book. Don't stop here. Continue getting to know yourself and learning about what you value, enjoy, like, dislike, and need.

Fostering Appreciation

Sometimes it can be easier to identify something you like in someone else before you can see it within yourself. People tend to be much kinder when evaluating others than when evaluating themselves. So what might be seen as a social deficit for you is seen as a social strength for someone else. Here you will identify differences that you appreciate in others before turning that lens toward yourself. Reflect on people you admire and identify at least one way their differences work to their benefit.

PERSON	BENEFICIAL DIFFERENCE
Greta Thunberg and Hannah Gadsby	Both have autism and credit this with their ability to succeed at public speaking and advocacy

Think of one way being an HSP makes you feel different from your peers (social, familial, professional, educational, etc.).

Being an HSP makes me feel different in this way: _____

_____

How do you feel about this difference?

_____

_____

_____

_____

How have you tried to minimize or avoid this difference?

_____

_____

_____

_____

What would happen if you accepted and embraced this difference?

_____

_____

_____

_____

If you let go of this worry, where can you allocate those resources instead?

_____

_____

_____

_____

Beginning to see the world through a lens of beneficial differences allows space for valuing diversity, including your own. Your differences make you unique; they are what will set you apart from others. How you interpret this can make a big difference in whether this is a hindrance or a gift.

SPIRITUALITY

HSPs tend to be more in tune with and affected by nature, faith, and spirituality. Depending on your cultural background, your experiences in organized religion, and what resonates with your lived experience, this sensitivity can take many forms. As is true in all aspects of an HSP's experience, faith has the possibility to be deeply wounding as well as immensely nurturing.

FAITH. The research between spirituality/faith and HSPs is lacking at this time; however, it is commonly reported anecdotally by HSPs as a significant part of their well-being. Combining knowledge of the overactivity of the central nervous system in HSPs, how mindfulness practices calm the CNS, and research documenting the benefits of mindfulness practices on mood disorders (Khusid and Vythilingam, 2016), it begins to make sense.

Many faiths and spiritual practices incorporate some form of meditation and mindfulness, often under the label of prayer, scripture memorizing, or singing. As such, spiritual practices often help calm the CNS. Practices like yoga can be particularly appealing, as they combine spiritual practices with bodywork. Making space in your life for spiritual practices that are nurturing to you benefits your mind, body, and soul.

NATURE. Many HSPs include nature as part of their spirituality. HSPs might make statements such as "I feel closest to God when I go camping" or "when I sit on the beach, I feel more connected to humanity." Similar to mindfulness, exposure to nature has been found to improve mood disorders and overall well-being (Pearson and Craig, 2014). This may be related to the reduced amount of sensory input that comes with being in nature, which can be soothing to an HSP. Nature is also often associated with less screen time, better air quality, and exposure to a variety of healthy bacteria. Having a pet can be another way of connecting with nature.

Spiritual Inventory

Many HSPs can identify the spiritual background they were raised in but struggle to identify what label they feel most comfortable with as an adult. The label tends to have minimal impact on the internal experience for you. Instead of focusing on labels for your spirituality, take a moment to reflect on *how* you connect spiritually.

» Where do you find sources of hope and strength when you feel discouraged?

_____

_____

_____

_____

» What brings about a sense of peace and comfort for you?

_____

_____

_____

_____

» Where do you find a sense of meaning or purpose?

_____

_____

_____

_____

» How do you connect with these personally?

_____

_____

_____

_____

» How do you connect with these communally?

_____

_____

_____

_____

» What have you carried with you from your childhood?

_____

_____

_____

_____

» What have you adjusted or changed from the belief system in which you were raised?

_____

_____

_____

_____

Knowing how you experience spirituality can help you connect to and maximize experiences within the faith structure that you practice. It can also help you connect to this resource even when you might struggle to find the "right label."

Field Trip

This exercise requires a little bit of travel, as it invites you to connect with nature. If you have limited mobility or limited access to nature, you might try a nearby park or a nature video. There are no spaces to write in to encourage you to be connected with the scenery around you. Use these questions as prompts for your internal experience.

Start with a few deep breaths, breathing into your diaphragm and feeling your stomach rise and fall. Take in the fresh air and notice any scents of nature that might surround you.

Close your eyes and listen to the sounds of nature around you. What sounds do you notice that might get missed in the busyness of everyday life? Listen for a few minutes.

Move your attention to your source of spiritual connectedness and hope. Think of a word or short phrase from your belief system that will be your focus for the next few minutes.

Repeat this word or phrase each time you breathe in. Allow it to permeate your thoughts, your breath, your experience of the nature around you. You may take periods with your eyes open or closed, whichever helps you focus and connect with nature.

End your time with a statement (prayer, intention, mantra—whatever fits best for you) of gratitude for this time of slow, meditative reflection. Carry this word or phrase with you for the remainder of your week.

Connecting with nature and things outside of yourself can be grounding or centering, especially for HSPs.

IDENTIFYING MY NEEDS

Hopefully, you have learned about yourself through the course of this book. In the spirit of embracing your differences and having compassion for your needs, begin thinking about what your needs are. When sensory and emotional needs get moved from the "optional" category into the "necessary" category, HSPs will often start engaging them differently. In the same way that you might need to take medication every day (like an antihistamine) and have emergency medication (like a rescue inhaler), there are certain life adjustments that you need every day to maintain your optimal functioning or adapt to unexpected triggers. Like medication, you may occasionally miss a "dose," and that might be for something you value (e.g., staying out late and knowing you will be tired for a few days) or something unavoidable (e.g., traveling), but for best results, follow your guidelines as closely as possible.

Understanding Needs

Thinking back on the topics from this book, take time to identify three helpful rules or interventions to optimize your functioning in the following domains. These may change over time. That's good—it means you are growing and changing. Some of them may be idealistic, so be compassionate with yourself and others when these are not attainable. Begin outlining your needs below.

Environmental needs (consider the five senses):

1. _____
   _____

2. _____
   _____

3. _____
   _____

4. _____
   _____

5. _____
   _____

What I need in social environments to engage well:

1. _____
   _____

2. _____
   _____

3. _____
   _____

What I need in conflict conversations to move toward repair:

1. _____

_____

2. _____

_____

3. _____

_____

What I need in a romantic relationship to feel safe:

1. _____

_____

2. _____

_____

3. _____

_____

What I need to be my best self around my family:

1. _____

_____

2. _____

_____

3. _____

_____

What I need to function best at work:

1. _____
   _____

2. _____
   _____

3. _____
   _____

What I need for my health:

1. Nutritional all-stars: _____
   _____

2. Nutritional disrupters: _____
   _____

3. Exercise regimen: _____
   _____

4. Amount of sleep: _____
   _____

5. _____
   _____

My go-to interventions when feeling overstimulated:

1. At home: _____

_____

2. At work: _____

_____

3. In social settings: _____

_____

4. _____

_____

5. _____

_____

Hold on to this list as a reminder of your needs. Update it every so often as you grow, as circumstances change, or as you understand your needs better.

CHAPTER RECAP

Deep work can be an ambiguous and confusing term. Keep in mind that all great accomplishments are done one step at a time. This chapter began to scratch the surface of deeper work. Return to these exercises as often as is helpful, and don't hesitate to ask for help in the healing process. There is a list of resources at the end of this book that can be particularly helpful in moving toward wholeness. Remember:

1. Healing is a painful and difficult process that will take time and can rarely be accomplished in isolation. Give yourself space to experience the process, and choose your company carefully.

2. Embracing your differences will open new doors to freedom, growth, and experiences.

3. Investing in yourself is worth the time, energy, and money. It will make you a better friend, partner, professional, family member, etc.

RESOURCES

BOOKS

The Highly Sensitive Person: How to Thrive When the World Overwhelms You by Elaine N. Aron, PhD. In this great introductory book to HSP, Dr. Aron provides a helpful place to start learning about the trait.

Wisdom from the Couch: Knowing and Growing Yourself from the Inside Out by Jennifer L. Kunst, PhD. Dr. Kunst speaks to common human experiences and the journey of therapy in a way that demystifies therapy. Dr. Kunst gets into the deeper processes of life that many HSPs often contemplate and process, making it a nice companion book for any HSP journey.

Quiet: The Power of Introverts in a World That Can't Stop Talking by Susan Cain. Ms. Cain covers many nuances to introversion that overlap well with HSP experiences. Since the majority of HSPs are introverts, it is a helpful expansion on the connection between the two traits.

PARASYMPATHETIC NERVOUS SYSTEM SUPPORT

INSIGHT TIMER. A meditation app with a large library of free guided meditations. The app offers a wide variety of length, style, and languages.

HEARTMATH. HeartMath is a biofeedback tool to help you learn how your breathing affects your heart and allows you to actively train your parasympathetic nervous system. There's a onetime cost for the device with free ongoing access to the app.

DOYOGAWITHME.COM. A large library of yoga videos of all lengths, styles, and difficulties. This website makes quality yoga exercise more accessible if cost or availability are limiting factors for you.

WEBSITE

HSPERSON.COM. Dr. Elaine Aron's website with links to additional HSP books, websites, videos, and professionals. Here you can find a list of coaches, therapists, and psychologists who work with HSPs and understand the trait.

REFERENCES

Acevedo, B. P., E. N. Aron, A. Aron, M.-D. Sangster, N. Collins, and L. L. Brown. "The Highly Sensitive Brain: An fMRI Study of Sensory Processing Sensitivity and Response to Others' Emotions." *Brain & Behavior* 4 (June 23, 2014): 580–94.

Aron, E. N. *The Highly Sensitive Child: Helping Our Children Thrive When the World Overwhelms Them.* New York: Harmony Books, 2002.

Aron, E. N. *The Highly Sensitive Person: How to Thrive When the World Overwhelms You.* New York: Birch Lane Press, 1996.

Aron, E. N. *Psychotherapy and the Highly Sensitive Person: Improving Outcomes for That Minority of People Who Are the Majority of Clients.* New York: Routledge, 2010.

Cain, S. *Quiet: The Power of Introverts in a World That Can't Stop Talking.* New York: Crown Publishers, 2012.

Goldberg, A., Z. Ebraheem, C. Freiberg, R. Ferarro, S. Chai, and O. D. Gottfried. "Sweet and Sensitive: Sensory Processing Sensitivity and Type 1 Diabetes." *Journal of Pediatric Nursing* 38 (January–February 2018): e35–e38.

Greeson, J. M., H. Zarrin, M. J. Smoski, J. G. Brantley, T. R. Lynch, D. M. Webber, M. H. Hall, E. C. Suarez, and R. Q. Wolever. 2018. "Mindfulness Meditation Targets Transdiagnostic Symptoms Implicated in Stress-Related Disorders: Understanding Relationships between Changes in Mindfulness, Sleep Quality, and Physical Symptoms." *Evidence-Based Complementary and Alternative Medicine* 2018 (May 13, 2018).

Greven, C. U., F. Lionetti, C. Booth, E. N. Aron, E. Fox, H. E. Schendan, M. Pluess, H. Bruining, B. Acevedo, P. Bijttebier, J. Homber. 2019. "Sensory Processing Sensitivity in the Context of Environmental Sensitivity: A Critical Review and Development of Research Agenda." *Neuroscience & Behavioral Reviews* 98 (March 2019): 287–305.

Khusid, M. A., and M. Vythilingam. "The Emerging Role of Mindfulness Meditation as Effective Self-Management Strategy, Part 1: Clinical Implications for Depression, Post-Traumatic Stress Disorder, and Anxiety." *Military Medicine* 181, no. 9 (September 2016): 961–68.

Kunst, J. L. *Wisdom from the Couch: Knowing and Growing Yourself from the Inside Out.* Las Vegas: Central Recovery Press, 2014.

Maté, G. *When the Body Says No: Exploring the Stress-Disease Connection.* Hoboken, NJ: John Wiley & Sons, Inc., 2003.

Newman, T. "All about the Central Nervous System." Last modified December 22, 2017.

Pearson, D. G., and T. Craig. 2014. "The Great Outdoors? Exploring the Mental Health Benefits of Natural Environments." *Frontiers in Psychology* 5 (October 21, 2014): 1178.

Pongratz, G., and R. H. Straub. "The Sympathetic Nervous Response in Inflammation." *Arthritis Research & Therapy* 16 (2014).

Van der Kolk, B. *The Body Keeps the Score: Brain, Mind, and Body in the Healing of Trauma.* New York: Penguin, 2014.

Yang, Y. C., C. Boen, K. Gerken, T. Li, K. Schorpp, and K. M. Harris. "Social Relationships and Physiological Determinants of Longevity across the Human Life Span." *Proceedings of the National Academy of Sciences* 113, no. 3 (January 2016): 578–83.

Yano, K., and K. Oishi. "The Relationships among Daily Exercise, Sensory-Processing Sensitivity, and Depressive Tendency in Japanese University Students." *Personality and Individual Differences* 127 (June 1, 2018): 49–53.

INDEX

A

advocate, as self, 12, 37, 58, 110, 133. *See also* self-advocacy
Aron, Elaine Dr., 3
assertiveness, 141–42

B

barriers, to emotional healing, 138–39
beliefs
  false, 79, 80–81
  reshaping, 81–82
blaming, self, 70
boundaries
  blurred, 101, 139
  challenges with, 68–69
  family relationships, within, 66
  friendships and, 77
  identifying, 65
  labeling, 67
  rules, as setting concise, 64, 141
budgeting, as time management, 21, 24–30

C

Cain, Susan, 5, 157
central nervous system (CNS), 17–18, 147

children
  boundaries and, 64–65, 72
  expectations and, 75
  HSP, living with, 6, 42–43, 139
  internalizing experiences, 42, 110
communication
  healthcare, as concerning, 110
  relationships, within, 56
conflict avoidance, 60
creating safe space, 57

D

deep thinker, qualities of, 2
deep work, meeting personal goals, 151–55
discovery exercises
  body, mindfulness of, 108–09
  boundary recognition, 65–66, 67–69
  childhood, reflection on, 43–46
  communication, effective, 54–56
  emotional healing, 138–39
  environmental assessment, 14
  expectations, managing in relationships, 77–78

feedback skills, assessing, 60–62
health, reflections on, 111–13
help, asking for, 58–59
lesson learned, 143–44
living space, changes to, 15–16
management, resource, 21
memory processing, 33–35, 71
movement, routines of, 114–16
nature, connection with, 150
nutrition, effects of, 124–25
relationship skills and, 51–53, 63
routine, establishing a, 31–32
self-care, as a priority, 16, 128, 129–30
self-compassion, learning, 46, 130, 135, 144
self-parenting, 140–42
shame game, letting go of, 143–44
social events, preparations for, 38–41
spiritual connections, 148–49
stimulation, assessing levels of, 17–19
time tracking charts, 24–30

E

Ehlers-Danlos syndrome
    (EDS), 106
emotional response, 139
    empathy, as, 4
    intense, defined as, 3
    managing, 57, 68, 77, 140
    processing,
        positively, 140–41
    recognizing value of,
        73, 76, 79
empath, 4
empathy, as emotional
    response, 3, 73, 79, 139
employment, advisers
    and, 90, 99
exercise
    needs, meeting
        personal, 151–54
expectations
    children, as beneficial for, 75
    identifying, 63, 68, 77, 93
    managing, 22, 60
    missed, as family, 70–71
    relationships,
        identifying in, 63
    social settings, in, 5
experiences
    building new, 134
extroverts, 4

F

family
    choice of, 70
    extended, 63, 74
    relationships with, 64

feedback, effective, 60
fitting in, feelings of
    not, 70, 144
friendships,
    contributions of, 76

G

gratitude, as a response, 3,
    56, 134, 150
grief, feelings of, 20, 134
guilt, feelings of, 20, 37, 57,
    113, 129

H

healthcare
    avoidance of, 110
    fight, flight, or freeze
        reaction to stress, 106
    medication and dosing, 110
    reflection, of the journey,
        110–13, 131
    self-awareness, as listening
        to your body, 107–09
    speaking up, as
        difficult, 110
help, asking for, 58
highly sensitive person (HSP)
    body, listening to as
        important, 107–108
    characteristics of, 2, 9
    checklist, as
        self-assessment, 7–8
    children, and, 6
    cultural ideals and, 5
    decision making, social
        events and, 37

environment and, 13
friendships and, 75
parenting, 72
social situations
    and, 35–36
stress, effects of, 106, 137
workplace strengths, 96–97

I

interventions
    children, with, 72–74
    therapeutic, 137
introverts, 4

K

Kunst, Jennifer Dr., 134

L

learning process,
    embracing, 143–44
LGBTQ, family of
    choice and, 70

M

Matè, Gabor Dr., 137
meditation, parasympathetic
    nervous system and, 106
memory recall, exercises
    for, 33–35
mindful practices
    meditation, 106, 126–127, 147
    social events, preparing
        for, 38–41
    yoga, 106, 147

N

needs
  communicating, 4, 12–13,
    42, 50–56
  identifying, 7, 12, 21,
    37, 40–43
negative outcomes, susceptible
  to, 32, 42
nutrition, charting, 117–23

O

Oishi, Kazuo, 106, 159
overstimulation
  balance, as in finding, 20
  characteristic of HSP, 2,
    12, 17, 47
  coping strategy, 18, 20, 47

P

parenting, challenges of, 72–74
perceptiveness, as increased
  awareness, 3
processing
  expectations, unmet, 71
  increased depth of, 2
  memories, 33

R

reflection, as to past
  experiences, 32, 42, 60
relationships
  communication and, 50, 54
  connection difficulties, 49

expectations, and, 63
false beliefs and, 79
family and, 64

S

self-advocacy, 42, 58, 103, 111
self-care, 11
  communication, as in
    listening to your
    body, 105
  empowering, as, 126–27
  limitations, consequences of
    ignoring, 114
  nutrition matters, 116
  parenting challenges, 72–74
  selfish, perceived as, 129
self-compassion
  practicing, 20, 72,
    134, 145–46
  understanding, 43, 46, 114,
    135, 144
sensitivities, self-care
  and, 126
sensory processing sensitivity
  (SPS), 3
sensory processing,
  defined as, 139
shame
  functional, as, 77, 144
  managing techniques, 57, 83
  overstimulation and, 20
  past, from the, 6
  people pleasing and, 42
  self-care needs, and,
    126, 129

shaming, as response to
  self-care, 126
social environments
  challenges of, 5, 11, 35–36
  functioning in, 151
spirituality, connection
  with, 147
stimulation
  optimal levels of, 17–18
  overwhelming, 2, 4
stress
  management, 13, 15–16,
    38, 98, 114
  physical presentation of,
    106, 137
  productive, as, 12
sympathetic nervous system,
  triggers to, 106

T

time management
  exercise for, 21, 23
  scheduling skills, 22
trauma, processing past, 65,
  102, 110, 140

V

validation, need for, 56,
  73, 103
van der Kolk, Bessel Dr., 137
visual processing,
  increased, 2

W

workplace
appreciation, obligation or, 94–95, 99–100
balancing needs, 85–86
feedback, reactions to, 93–94, 102
preferences, 90–91
strengths, assessment of, 96–97
stressors, 98, 101–102
values, as differing, 92
values, assessment of, 86–87, 88–89, 103

wounds, healing old, 134
wounds, unintentional, 70, 79

Y

Yano, Koske, 106, 159

ACKNOWLEDGMENTS

First and foremost, thank you to Ben, the first editor on everything I've ever written and my tireless cheerleader. I consider myself lucky every day. Words cannot express the appreciation I have for you.

Thank you to the strong women in my life who helped me with this project, each from within her own area of expertise and wisdom: Liz, Katie, Shin, Reba, Adrienne, Tiffany, Clara, Grace, Stefanie, Esther, Alex, and Amy. You have each continually supported me and my career, and I am blessed to know each one of you.

My career is built upon the shoulders of mentors who have each pushed me forward and held me up at different times, bringing me to this point. Thank you, Mari, Annie, Lee, Maria, and Kevin.

I could not have written this book without the ongoing support of my medical team, who keep my Zebra body functional. A few months ago, I would not have believed this book to be possible, but your tireless efforts have allowed me to keep pursuing my passion. Thank you all.

To my clients—it's an honor to walk alongside you in life. You are stronger and more impressive than you realize.

And finally, thank you to my team at Callisto for bringing this project and my dream of being an author to life. Specifically, thank you to Vanessa Ta and Patrick Castrenze. It would not exist without you all working behind the scenes to bring it into existence.

ABOUT THE AUTHOR

Amanda Cassil, PhD, (pronouns: she/her) is a licensed clinical psychologist based out of Pasadena, CA. She is the founder and CEO of STEM Psychological Services, providing psychological support to women and underrepresented minorities in STEM fields (science, technology, engineering, and math). This clinical focus has resulted in extensive experience with highly sensitive people as well as chronic illnesses and invisible disabilities. Dr. Cassil cofounded and cochairs the Feminist Special Interest Group for the San Gabriel Valley Psychological Association. For more information, visit STEMpsychology.com.

CPSIA information can be obtained
at www.ICGtesting.com
Printed in the USA
BVHW090900201020
591213BV00003B/3